My Amazing Transformation of
Love, Courage, and Wisdom

MARTY COLE

BALBOA.
PRESS

A DIVISION OF HAY HOUSE

Balboa Press books may be ordered through booksellers or by contacting:

Balboa Press
A Division of Hay House
1663 Liberty Drive
Bloomington, IN 47403
www.balboapress.com
1 (877) 407-4847

Because of the dynamic nature of the Internet, any web addresses or
links contained in this book may have changed since publication and may
no longer be valid. The views expressed in this work are solely those
of the author and do not necessarily reflect the views of the publisher,
and the publisher hereby disclaims any responsibility for them.

The author of this book does not dispense medical advice or prescribe the use
of any technique as a form of treatment for physical, emotional, or medical
problems without the advice of a physician, either directly or indirectly. The
intent of the author is only to offer information of a general nature to help you
in your quest for emotional and spiritual well-being. In the event you use any
of the information in this book for yourself, which is your constitutional right,
the author and the publisher assume no responsibility for your actions.

Any people depicted in stock imagery provided by Thinkstock are models,
and such images are being used for illustrative purposes only.
Certain stock imagery © Thinkstock.

Print information available on the last page.

ISBN: 978-1-5043-8815-3 (sc)
ISBN: 978-1-5043-8817-7 (hc)
ISBN: 978-1-5043-8816-0 (e)

Library of Congress Control Number: 2017914411

Balboa Press rev. date: 02/16/2017

Dedication

I dedicate this book to my father, Dr. Harvey J. Cole, who inspired me with his wisdom.

I love you, Dad.

Contents

Foreword

I was shocked and honored when my dear friend Marty called me out of the blue and asked me to help him with his book. My response? "Oh, my God!" I had met Marty about seven years earlier at our HeartMath class at Unity of Tustin. We discovered our many synchronicities: Both of our mothers were named Dorothy, were born in 1916, and died weeks apart at the age of 94. We lived a couple of miles apart in north Orange County. We both have loved meditation since 1975. And we have read many of the same authors and helped the homeless.

I have been a guest at Marty's Cal State Fullerton OLLI class. For his last Wisdom Healing Circle gathering, a poetry night, I recited my ode to Marty, which appears after this forward. This poem, like this book, shows how Marty walks his spiritual self-improvement talk. He is love in action, the most generous, tender soul. Marty writes like he talks—positively, passionately, and lovingly. After you read his touching story, you will have more compassion for him and for yourself. And, no, I was never in his mixed fruit salad bowl.

—Patti Higgins, friend

To those who know Marty, his name is synonymous with the word *love*. That's the essence of who Marty is. He breathes love and spreads love. He touches everyone—strangers, friends, and loved ones—with his love. He is the warmest and most caring person I have ever known. He cares deeply about our planet and loves to inspire others to make a contribution to this world

Surprisingly, the Marty we know today is not the Marty his friends once knew. The pages in this book will reveal how he rose above his physical and inner struggles in life to become a beacon of light to others. I have been blessed to see Marty's metamorphosis into what and where he is today. Through the years, he and I have inspired each other with the wisdom we have learned from life, along with our passion for music.

I am the rainbow turtle Marty talks about in this book. Wonder where I got my name? Marty takes pride in telling me that I give color and meaning to his life, and like a turtle, he appreciates my calm inner strength as I swim through this sea called life.

I have known Marty to be fearless in his quest for truth. Like a rhino, he is strong in what he stands for, believing in us and the best that we can be. Marty's story is empowering, uplifting, and a living miracle of love, courage, and wisdom.

Namaste.

—Rainbow Turtle, Musician

Marty

Baseball hat, talking
To rhinos and lighthouses
Sacred bowls singing his beat of
Miracles, poetry, and positivity
Eating chocolates and soaped up
On once-white carpet
Stained with bejeweled hearts
As dancers hula,
Shamans chant and all laugh along.
What an IONS adventure he fearlessly leads
Monthly communing his Cheyenne space.
To wisdom victories,
Don Miguel, Mercy House, Abraham, and Louise.
Our persistent, giving friend,
Fathering action,
Our OLLI prof walks his taught talk,
We circle our beloved Marty,
For a decade past and forever on,
With our deepest thanks.

Reprinted with the permission of the author, Patti Higgins, written for Marty Cole's last Wisdom Healing Circle poetry night on February 15, 2016.

Preface

I hope, my readers, you are empowered with my wisdom. I am a passionate and enthusiastic person who wants to get my ideas across to you. I feel that I am a mirror, a magnet to other people and our world. I am attracted to, and attract to me, positive and aware people. I want the best out of life for myself and others.

My life has had a lot of surprising experiences, and I want you to learn from them. I value getting the most conscious self-help and establishing relationships with the most aware people possible.

I am so grateful that I have been blessed and that I have prospered so that I have been able to surround myself with the top teachers in their fields. I want to share my transformational life journey with you. Our planet needs us to wake up and to love, not fear.

—Marty Cole, February 2017

Acknowledgments

Some of the people I want to acknowledge are mentioned in this book and even quoted (with their permission). I love using quotations in my writing; they help us remember who we are. My references to these master teachers come from my excellent memory of my eighteen-year spiritual journey and from my copious notes from lectures, classes, conferences, and workshops. I have asked permission from these wonderful people to quote them. I gratefully acknowledge their kindnesses to me and their contributions to this work. To those angels and spirit guides on the other side, I thank them for watching out for us.

Phil and Lori Cole, Steve Cole, Mike and Leah Cole, Vicky Cole, Sarah Cole, Melissa Cole, Dr. Harvey Cole, Dorothy Cole, Bobby and Nanci Cole, Gary and Claudette Cole, Adele Cole, Dr. Leonard Cole, Joyce Morris, Aurora Belderol, Derek Gable, Richard Sherman, Steve and Linda Shraeder, Alan Morris, Aeyrie Silver Eagle, Kate Marrs, Bob and Linda Strickler, Bob Morris, Carol White, Caroline Lee, Dick and Tammie Golden, Judy Smith, Dr. Robert Landman, Fred Afshar, Gary Mergotti, Libbie

Amsell, Margie Andrews, Lowell Dellalba, Helen Delaney and Family, Ileen Levine, Jacqueline Wilson, Jan Cogan, Jill Kimbrell, Jim Kashiwada and family, Don Hutchinson, Jonathan Yoon, Jon Claude Pinot, Ken and MaryAnn Luehman, Larry Haynes, Liz Lincoln, Lovely Linda, Tony and Lulu Williams, Marci Matthews, Marjorie Gibson, Mark Geller, Marla Greer, Mary Johnson, Master Mingtong Gu, Dr. Edgar Mitchell, Meredith Laskow, Mia and Larry Humphreys, Monica Mandle, Bruce and Nan Cole, David Cole and his partner, Steve, Barbara and David Mann, Patti Higgins, Chris Higgins, David J. Brooks, Brahms, Phil Kaus, Prany Sananikone, Randy Polevoi, Renee Elkins, George Trivich, Cindy and Brian Rouze, Roger and Barbara Switzsky, Ron and Naomi Jue, Ron Duben, Roz and Steve Alford, Sandy and Linda Freud, Sandy Opperman, Sharon Levey, Sigrun Borneo, Sueda Rao, Thoma, Tim Praskins, Val and Rolanda Engstrom, Wen Daniels, David Cortez, Carolyn Cardoni, Chris Levine, Daniel O'Hara, Mariana Fischer-Militataru, David Morris, Shirley Morris, Alan and Jill Morris, Diane Morris, David Grant Wright, Lorenzo Caunan, Patty DeFrancis, Erin Moran, Erin Armstrong, Pam and all the doctors at UCLA who saved my life two times, Esther Rabinowitz, Thich Nhat Hanh, Dr James Q. Simmons III, Scott Alexander, Dr. Wayne Dyer, Don Miguel Ruiz, John R. Wooden, Tom Hopkins, J. Douglas Edwards, Albert Einstein, the Dalai Lama, Colin Powell, Eckhart Tolle, Dr. Bruce Lipton, Brendon Burchard, Jon Kabat-Zinn, Lao Tzu, Dr. Arnold Beckman, LeVar Burton, all the people at IONS, especially Andrea Livingston, all the people at CSUF OLLI, Nelson Mandela, the Beatles, the writers and teachers of *A Course in Miracles*, Dr. Lynne D. Kitei, Kareem Abdul-Jabbar, Michael Warren, Kenny Heitz, Lucius Allen, and Lynn Shackelford, The Doors, Whitney Houston, HeartMath, Doc Childre, Esther and Jerry Hicks, Marianne Williamson, Maharishi Yogi, Dr. Jean Houston, Dr. Dean Radin, Dr. Marilyn Schlitz, Kathleen Erickson Freeman, Dr. Sigmund Freud, Haile Selassie, Lady Gaga, Michael Jackson, Queen, Joe Cocker, Robert T. Kiyosaki, Deborah Jones, and saving the best for the last, I acknowledge that I am grateful for myself, Marty Cole.

Chapter 1

What I Learned Growing Up

I am very grateful for this moment in my life—right here, right now.

Life has been very good to me, and I live in gratitude every day. Everything that has happened to me is for my benefit, for the benefit of others, and for my highest good.

I began my journey on September 17, 1953. I was born in Santa Monica, California, and grew up in Palos Verdes Peninsula. My father, Harvey, was an orthodontist, and my mother, Dorothy, was a teacher, artist, and homemaker. I have two older brothers, Michael and Steven, and a younger brother, Philip.

I went away to military school at the tender age of six. Living in a military school taught me to have character and discipline, to be neat and organized, and to respect people. What I appreciated the most was learning sports. I played football, basketball, baseball, and tennis. Sports taught me to develop my skills, to be competitive, and to coordinate my mind and body. They also helped me channel my energy in a positive way.

When I transferred schools at twelve and thirteen years old, I was finally introduced to girls. I really enjoyed girls. They were beautiful, fun, and sweet, and they liked to flirt with me. I started to find what I thought of as "love" for the first time. It was wonderful! Girls made me feel good about myself and were very playful to be around. I went steady with many girls in the eighth grade.

At this time in my life, I started to love myself for the first time with the help of a counselor at UCLA, Dr. James Q. Simmons III. He was the most loving and caring person I had ever met and was so compassionate and kind to me.

When I returned home at fifteen, I had a difficult time adjusting to home life after nine years away. I asked my father if I could get my own apartment. I'll never forget his words: "No problem, son. I'll get you your own place to live." And he did.

I moved into the apartment above my dad's dental office in Redondo Beach, California. For the first time in my life, I had freedom. The wisdom here is that freedom is a very important thing. We should never take it for granted. To have freedom was the most important thing in my life at that time, because it was a new experience.

It was perfect timing for me. This was the late 1960s and early 1970s when there was more rebellion and major sexual freedom. It was the time of free love and flower power. I couldn't have asked for a better time to be a teenager. Life was amazing.

I'm grateful for the music group the Beatles; their music changed the world and my life forever. People became freer.

I fell in true love for the first time with a girl named Cherry. She was beautiful, sexy, and wore hot pants and fishnets, which were very popular back then. Hot pants were short shorts and very inviting to be close to, if you know what I mean.

When I moved to Torrance, California, Cherry and I broke up. Then I met Brandy and enrolled in El Camino College. Brandy and I broke up all the time, but I was deeply in love with her. However, during these breakups, many girls came to my apartment and asked if I wanted to be their boyfriend. I would always say yes. Back then, yes was the magic word. When I said yes, they would say, "Let's go to bed!"

The sexual revolution was really heating up. I had thirty-five girlfriends over a couple years. I'm not kidding. Sex was easy, and all the girls were on birth control pills. Sex was everywhere and everything to me. I had wild parties every weekend with sex all around me. It was amazing that all this was happening to me. When I had sex, I felt validation. It was like I was totally accepted and appreciated by someone. The wisdom here is that both men and women just want to be accepted and appreciated.

I felt completely valued with girlfriends named Randy, Mandy, Apple, Cherry, Jeri, and Candy. Today, my soul mate's name is Rainbow Turtle. She calls all my old girlfriends a "mixed fruit-salad of girls." How do you like that title?

To date, I've had more than 150 girlfriends. Some were serious, but most were casual sexual partners. I'm not bragging; it's just a fact. I learned that women are a lot of fun to be with. But I recommend being careful what you ask for; you might get more than you bargained for.

I have no regrets in my life. Everything happens for a reason. There are no accidents or coincidences. Everything happens to us for three purposes:

1. To learn
2. To grow
3. To heal

Everything in our lives should be about these three important things, and again, everything happens in our lives to benefit us.

I transferred to California State University Dominguez Hills (CSUDH), where I got my bachelor of science degree in public administration in 1976. Sports were very important to me throughout school, and I lettered on the varsity tennis team both in high school and at CSUDH. I'm very proud of these accomplishments, as I'm the only person in my family to be on a starting team in collegiate sports. I also enjoyed traveling the western United States, eating the best food, staying in nice hotels, and playing competitive tennis at a high level.

I played tennis for thirty-six years, and it brought me a lot of fun and friends. My tennis experience continued when I was in my forties and played for the United States Tennis Association (USTA) and was ranked second-best player in Southern California in level 4.0.

There are seven levels of competitive tennis: level 1.0 is beginner, level 2.0 is advanced beginner, level 3.0 is intermediate, level 4.0 is advanced tennis. The most advanced level, 7.0, is the level in which Roger Federer, Andy Murray, Rafael Nadal, and the best players in the world compete. I did very well at my level. I played thirty tennis tournaments in one year, with four matches in each tournament, and I won eighteen finals in 1997 and 1998. For eighteen months, during these years, my record was seventy-two wins and five losses.

I'm grateful I got to play sports, especially tennis.

Prior to playing tennis, in my 30's, I was married twice and

5

have two beautiful daughters, Sarah and Melissa. They are the loves of my life. I'm very proud of them, and they are doing very well in their lives.

My life has been blessed, but it has not been without its ups and downs. I recently went to see the musical *Matilda*, and watching this play stirred up many thoughts and emotions in me, which I feel a strong desire to share with you. *Matilda* is about a special girl who is smart and loves to read. Her parents are mean and cold and don't give her any love. They are verbally, emotionally, psychologically, physically, and mentally abusive. Matilda also went to a very strict private school, similar to a military school. The principal was brutal and verbally and physically abusive.

When I was in military school from age six to eleven, I was severely verbally, physically, emotionally, mentally, and psychologically abused. I was beaten badly many times. I had welts and was often bloodied. If people would perform this kind of abuse in schools or elsewhere today, they would be put in jail.

Let's be thankful there are child-abuse laws today to protect children. I have forgiven these people for how they treated me. I have also forgiven all the bullies who picked on me.

Forgiveness is a very powerful healing modality. My hope here is that people will forgive those in their lives who have hurt them. Remember, people do not know what they do. They are usually taught bad behavior by other people or sometimes act that way because they didn't get enough attention or love from others. The wisdom here again is that it's all about love and love is all there is.

When I was sixteen and eighteen years of age, respectively, two different men raped me. One was a friend of my family; the other was a friend of mine. This was very hurtful to me, and I felt totally violated. But the counseling I have had over the years helped in my healing process.

Again, what I learned from these painful experiences is to forgive. I forgave these two men. Individuals like them are often lost souls who are not getting enough love from others, and they feel empty and lonely. My hope is that people report any kind of abuse to the proper authorities and seek professional counseling to help them with their issues. Love heals all people, places, and things if you believe it will.

The first time I was raped, a family friend who was invited to a family wedding celebration got me very drunk with thirteen glasses of champagne. He then took me to a back bedroom at the host's home, where the reception was being held. This person raped me repeatedly for several hours while I was practically passed out from all the alcohol he had forced on me. I had to go to the doctor a few days later to get my private area treated for lacerations. I did not report this attack because I felt very ashamed and guilty. I thought I was a bad boy and that I deserved it. I had very low self-esteem.

I did not tell anybody about being raped by this man until twenty-five years later. I told my three brothers at my home during a twenty-eight-hour discussion about the issues and conflicts we had with each other. When I told them how their "family friend" had violated me, they were shocked and could not believe it. After hearing the truth of my attack, they said that they were going to go to San Francisco and kill this pedophile. (They meant that figuratively, not literally, of course.)

The second sexual attack occurred two years later. I had this "friend" who happened to be gay, and I knew he had that lifestyle. I had just gotten very sick from a Caribbean cruise I had gone on with my parents. My temperature was 104 degrees from a virus I had contracted.

This guy called me and asked if he could come over to take care of me. I said no, but he insisted on coming to my house. I told him that he could come over on only one condition: that he promise to *not* come on to me *and* respect me for being a straight man. He promised to honor my boundaries. As soon as he came over to my apartment, he then raped me, and I could not defend myself because I was so very weak and sick.

I accept, honor, and respect gay, lesbian, and transgender people. I love everyone, no matter the lifestyle they choose. People who force others to have sex with them without their consent and against their will are unaware of the life-changing impact of their behavior. The moral of this story is that, though in no way do I agree with what they did, I do forgive the two men who raped me. I especially forgive myself in these traumatic experiences. Anyone who is going through these kinds of unfortunate events should seek counseling. I did, and it helped me get through it.

I also learned that if you are physically, mentally, emotionally, sexually, or psychologically abused, please report it to the police, your parents, teachers, and counselors. If you are bullied at school, please tell the school officials. My wisdom here is to encourage you to have the courage to report any abuse to the proper authorities. Have courage. Do not live in fear. Empower and love yourself!

Chapter 2

What I Learned in My Career

In my career, I was a salesman for eleven different companies. I am most proud of my role in helping start the first solar energy business in 1977. I was the first representative hired in the United States to sell solar energy and pioneered this field.

Look at it today: solar energy is the fastest growing industry in the United States. It is growing at 30 percent a year. In 2017, the field had 300,000 workers employed. The average solar hourly wage was $26.00 per hour. Solar jobs are exploding to one in fifty jobs in the United States labor market. Just take a look around at all the solar panels. Solar is surpassing the wind power industry. I am very honored to have been involved in the industry's start, and I am very proud of how far the industry has come.

A book I read in 1980 called *Rhinoceros Success* by Scott Alexander changed my life forever. This book became my Bible—the most important book of my life. It gave me courage, strength, and motivation to believe in myself, that I could set goals and accomplish anything and everything in my life. The book is so simple yet so deep and meaningful to me. It lit a fire under me, just like the Door's song "Light My Fire." My career exploded! I became the top salesperson in the world in the solar energy field for Reynolds Aluminum, which is now Alcoa.

While selling solar and playing tennis, I had another miracle! When I was playing tennis at my club, I met Derek Gable, who changed my life forever. Derek is a distinguished gentleman with an English accent. We became friends in 1977 and are still friends today.

Derek has had a very successful career with Mattel Toys, where he contributed to the creation of the *Masters of the Universe* toys—the main character was He-Man—which earned several billions of dollars of sales for Mattel. Using his very creative mind, he has patented hundreds of inventions over the years.

Derek came to me one day in 1992 and said, "Why don't you have a get-together with your three brothers and discuss any issues and resolve any conflicts." He said that having an open family discussion could be very helpful in bringing the family together. I took his advice, and we held an intensive communication event with my brothers at my house for twenty-eight hours straight, without breaks except for meals. A lot of good came out of it because there were more issues between us than we realized.

The wisdom I learned from this is that when we have conflicts with family members, coworkers, or friends, it is a great idea to hold a major communication meeting to resolve disagreements and create closer personal and business relationships. Increased cooperation and harmony can come out of these experiences. As you can see, I am very grateful for Derek and his ability to bring people and families together.

Another Derek-related story happened in 1993. Again, this brilliant man came to me and asked if we could have a meeting with my father, Dr. Harvey Cole; my mother, Dorothy; and my brothers about the possibility of developing a family business. Previously, whenever my brothers or I had asked our dad about the future possibility of a family business, he would always say, "Well, sons, I will take it under advisement," which meant, "No, it's not going to happen." However, when Derek communicated with my father, he listened and agreed on a family meeting.

We met at the Embassy Suites in Irvine, California, for five to six hours. The meeting was successful. My father became very interested, and several years later, my three brothers and I became a business partner with my father and mother in a family-owned shopping center in Flagstaff, Arizona. My dad's decision was based on Derek's findings, business, and personal experience, which convinced him that we as a family could have the opportunity to become closer as a family. My father was also influenced by his the advice of his personal attorney and certified public accountant.

This was the difference maker, the defining moment that. We became the Cole Family Partners for life. I learned from this amazing experience that when miracles come to you, you should take action and make it happen. Miracles are everywhere; we just need to pay attention and be aware and *take action*. I hope you will act on the miracles that happen in your life.

The next story is not a dream. It is a true and real story that happened to me. In July of 1985, I won a trip to Hawaii for being the company's number one salesman out of 40,000 employees. I invited my girlfriend to go with me. One night on the trip, we went to a movie in Maui. When we were driving back to our hotel around midnight, it was very dark, with no lights along the highway, which ran through the inner island. We both looked over to the right side of the highway and saw the most unusual sight I had ever seen: an unidentified flying object (UFO). Around 100 feet wide and about 150 feet tall, it was hovering thirty feet off the ground and making a very high-pitched humming noise. Bright white lights covered the spacecraft.

We pulled over, got out of the car, and walked closer, trying to get a better look.

As we neared, the humming got louder and louder. We were both very afraid. The UFO had a tremendous amount of energy and power. We were so frightened that we looked at each other and said we needed to get the hell out of there. We ran as fast as we could back to my car and split. I swear to God that we saw a UFO. We were very lucky to have gotten out of there okay.

We read in the Maui newspaper the next day that there had been major sightings of UFOs the night before in the same documented area. Well, what does that tell you about what we saw that night? I definitely believe in UFOs and extraterrestrial beings. I believe there is life outside our Planet Earth.

The wisdom here is to have an open mind and heart. I believe all things are possible" We only know 5 percent of what science has proven. That means 95 percent is unknown. Let us be open to the possibilities of more peace and love on this Planet Earth, in our solar system, and beyond.

Another documented UFO sighting occurred on January 22, 1997, though not by me. Dr. Lynne D. Kitei, MD, saw UFOs outside her window in Phoenix, Arizona. She wrote a book called *The Phoenix Lights* about her experience.

On March 13, 1997, at twilight, my friend Mary Ellen saw

two orange-amber ball-shaped UFOs fly very quickly across her sky in northern Arizona, heading southwest toward Phoenix, Arizona. Later that night, thousands of people, including Arizona's governor, saw a triangle of *hundreds* of UFOs traveling across the sky with bright white lights. This is all documented and filmed, and people took lie detector tests and passed, which confirms all of these events and encounters with UFOs.

I believe in UFOs and extraterrestrials 100 percent. Again, I keep an open heart, mind, and spirit and believe that all people, places, things, and aliens are possible. Be open to the possibilities in life. You will be amazed at what you will learn, how you will grow and heal, and what you will find.

Chapter 3

What Motivated Me in My Life

All my life, I have been motivated by three main empowering energies that I want to share with you. I have found that *symbols*, *mentors*, and *words* best motivate me to take action to improve my attitude and my life. You will notice mentions of these three activators throughout this book.

I have already mentioned a few of the great mentors who have inspired me, and there are more to come. Often they inspire me with their words, either in books, speeches, lectures at conferences, or—best of all—in person. I take excellent notes to help me remember what is so wisely stated. My house is filled with signs, plaques, and notes to remind me of their wisdom teachings.

Then there are the empowering symbols. Symbols give me strength, power, and courage that all things are possible, that I am fearless, and that I have no fear to talk to anyone or do anything to be successful, no matter how difficult it is. The wisdom here is that symbols are a very important part of my life.

My favorite animal spirit is the rhino. To me, the rhino symbolizes wisdom and courage and perseverance. I have more than three thousand rhinos in my home. One was woven in Africa and is bigger than a small horse. Guess where he resides? Beside my bed! I chose this symbol to empower me after reading Scott Alexander's *Rhinoceros Success*. Since reading this book, I have purchased well over one thousand copies to give to dear people I want to inspire. I have met this talented author several times and consider him a friend.

The other symbol that is very important to me is the lighthouse, a symbol of guidance, hope, faith, security, protection, and service to others. Do you know why I *love* lighthouses? Because all they do is serve others and expect nothing. Unlike most people, places, and things, they have no agenda. Lighthouses just serve. Plus, they are beautiful structures in the most lovely ocean settings in the world. I have a collection of three thousand lighthouses. I also love to visit them, and friends buy me lighthouse souvenirs on their trips. I think you should all understand the power of symbols in my life and what they represent to me.

I recommend that you too, create symbols in your life to which you can relate and that give you power, knowledge, hope, faith, love, gratitude, courage, determination, wisdom, and a whatever-it-takes attitude to do the very best you are capable of and nothing less.

My motto in life has been, "Whatever it takes to be successful, I will do it, no excuses." As Wayne Dyer says, "Excuses be gone! The average person has fifteen excuses not to do anything." I love Wayne Dyer. He has been my teacher, mentor, coach, and friend, as well as a beautiful spiritual leader of metaphysics and human development.

From my youth, I have been a magnet for meeting famous people who became my mentors, my heroes, and my motivators. I still have my childhood autograph collection of more than 250 autographs of famous actors, actresses, and musicians. I knew at a young age that there was a lot to learn from super successful people so I could become the best I could be. I want to meet mentors and learn from them, so I am attracted to high achievers.

I make a point of going to where my mentors speak and then talking with them after the event. When appropriate, I invite them to lunch or try to arrange some one-on-one time. After seeing and talking with me at several of their events, they start to remember me and what I do. I love it when we become friends. Please learn from my example.

> *Success is peace of mind attained only through self-satisfaction in knowing you made the effort to do the best of which you're capable.*
> —UCLA Coach John Wooden, Pyramid of Success

Another super motivator I have had in my life has been John Wooden, the UCLA basketball coach who was voted the greatest coach in any sport, in any level in the history of sports. Coach Wooden always said, "Do the very best you are capable of in your life." I met John Wooden three times. He always inspired me to be the best I could be. I love his Pyramid of Success model. It presents very powerful words of accomplishments to strive for in your life.

I met all of John Wooden's winning UCLA Bruins team—Lew Alcindor (now known as Kareem Abdul-Jabbar), Michael Warren, Kenny Heitz, Lucius Allen, and Lynn Shackelford. They won the NCAA 1967 basketball championship. My brother Mike knew Michael Warren from their fraternity. Mike introduced me to all these stars at a UCLA game. That was such a thrill for me.

Here are my favorite words from a program I got at a UCLA basketball game. They were taken from John Wooden's Pyramid of Success, a model for life that he created:

- *Confidence*—Respect without fear. May come from being prepared and keeping all things in proper perspective.
- *Team spirit*—A genuine consideration for others. An eagerness to sacrifice personal interests of glory for the welfare of all.
- *Alertness*—Be observing constantly. Stay open-minded. Be eager to learn and improve.
- *Industriousness*—There is no substitute for work. Worthwhile results come from hard work and careful planning.
- *Cooperation*—With all levels of your coworkers. Listen if you want to be heard. Be interested in finding the best way, not in having your own way.
- *Enthusiasm*—Brushes off upon those with whom you come in contact. You must truly enjoy what you are doing.

John Wooden really inspired me. His memory and wisdom will live on forever. See his complete Pyramid of Success model at www.woodencourse.com.

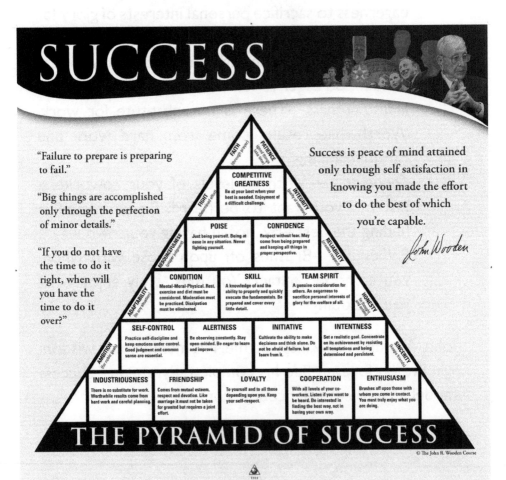

SUCCESS

"Failure to prepare is preparing to fail."

"Big things are accomplished only through the perfection of minor details."

"If you do not have the time to do it right, when will you have the time to do it over?"

Success is peace of mind attained only through self satisfaction in knowing you made the effort to do the best of which you're capable.

John Wooden

FAITH (through prayer)

PATIENCE (good things take time)

COMPETITIVE GREATNESS
Be at your best when your best is needed. Enjoyment of a difficult challenge.

FIGHT (determined effort)

INTEGRITY (purity of intention)

POISE
Just being yourself. Being at ease in any situation. Never fighting yourself.

CONFIDENCE
Respect without fear. May come from being prepared and keeping all things in proper perspective.

RESOURCEFULNESS (proper judgment)

RELIABILITY (respect earned)

CONDITION
Mental-Moral-Physical. Rest, exercise and diet must be considered. Moderation must be practiced. Dissipation must be eliminated.

SKILL
A knowledge of and the ability to properly and quickly execute the fundamentals. Be prepared and cover every little detail.

TEAM SPIRIT
A genuine consideration for others. An eagerness to sacrifice personal interests of glory for the welfare of all.

ADAPTABILITY (to any situation)

HONESTY (in thought and action)

SELF-CONTROL
Practice self-discipline and keep emotions under control. Good judgment and common sense are essential.

ALERTNESS
Be observing constantly. Stay open-minded. Be eager to learn and improve.

INITIATIVE
Cultivate the ability to make decisions and think alone. Do not be afraid of failure, but learn from it.

INTENTNESS
Set a realistic goal. Concentrate on its achievement by resisting all temptations and being determined and persistent.

AMBITION (for noble goals)

SINCERITY (keeps friends)

INDUSTRIOUSNESS
There is no substitute for work. Worthwhile results come from hard work and careful planning.

FRIENDSHIP
Comes from mutual esteem, respect and devotion. Like marriage it must not be taken for granted but requires a joint effort.

LOYALTY
To yourself and to all those depending upon you. Keep your self-respect.

COOPERATION
With all levels of your co-workers. Listen if you want to be heard. Be interested in finding the best way, not in having your own way.

ENTHUSIASM
Brushes off upon those with whom you come in contact. You must truly enjoy what you are doing.

THE PYRAMID OF SUCCESS

© The John R. Wooden Course

JOHN R. WOODEN
COURSE
www.woodencourse.com

My other motivators and teachers were Tom Hopkins and J. Douglas Edwards, lecturers and authors of *Mastering the Art of Selling* and *Closing the Sales*. They both told me the most important question is the "Alternate of Choice Closing Question." For example, "Would you prefer red or blue?" or "Would you like your product or services this Wednesday or Thursday?" They would always tell me to ask questions and then *be quiet*. I grossed $20 million in sales using this technique. I truly was a born salesman and was very successful doing it for thirty years.

Chapter 4

Getting Cancer Changed My Life Forever

It was 1999 and I was the top salesperson of the year for Life Alert Company with their "I have fallen and I can't get up" medical alert devices. I was married with two small daughters, ages nine and four. I was playing competitive tennis for the United States Tennis Association. I played thirty tournaments that year and won eighteen. I was ranked number two in Southern California. My marriage was not going well, and I played tennis four hours a day, seven days a week just to stay away from my wife at the time.

I played a very tough tournament in Whittier Narrows. I was in the final set for three long hours and lost 6-3,

3-6, and 4-6. After the game, I was very tired and sensed something pop in my neck. I felt my neck and found a huge swollen lymph node on the left side. Frequently, neck cancer first manifests on the left side. I went to visit my mom and dad in La Jolla, California. My parents told me to go to the doctor and have it checked out.

I went to my doctor, who said it was a cyst. "Take these antibiotics and I will see you in two weeks," he said. The follow-up appointment showed no improvement. The lymph node had just become more inflamed and swollen. My doctor referred me to a head and neck surgeon. I went to the new doctor, and he eyeballed me with his hands and eyes and said, "I think you have a nine-centimeter, a tennis ball sized, tumor in your neck. You need to go to the hospital now for a biopsy immediately."

I was put under anesthesia, and the doctor took out a piece of my neck. One week later, after the pathology report came back, my doctor said I had a stage IV squamous cell carcinoma in my left neck. Just to clarify, stage V is six feet under, which means you are dead. The doctor said I had a 90 percent chance of dying within one year. Of course, I was devastated. I got down from the examination table in the doctor's office and fell into a fetal position in a corner of the room. I could not believe what had just happened. In one minute, my life had been changed forever.

The doctor explained to me that I needed a nineteen-hour surgery to remove 50 percent of my neck, including my tongue, vocal cords, and muscles, and nerves. He was reading from a medical book dated 1985 to treat my cancer. The research was fourteen years out of date!

Next he said, "The operation is so intensive, I will need a helper to cut half your neck off." The doctor also explained that no person who'd had this procedure had lived past five years. Also, he was going to give me radiation and chemotherapy. I was so scared and afraid. I called my family members, and they were devastated and traumatized by my condition.

My brother Mike and sister-in-law Leah had connections at the UCLA Medical Center in Los Angeles. They spent hours on the phone trying to get me to the best second opinion possible. They got me a great doctor, the chief of head and neck surgery. To this day, I am very grateful for what Mike and Leah did for me.

The new doctor said I did not need a nineteen-hour surgery. What I needed was a tonsillectomy to remove my tonsils, three months of radiation, two months of chemotherapy in the hospital, and then hopefully, a modified neck dissection afterward.

I had a very hard time dealing with this diagnosis, as I was very scared. My brother Steve was very loving and supportive and came to visit me from Santa Barbara, where he lives. He visited and stayed with me overnight in the hospital. I will always appreciate my brothers' love and support.

My cousins Bruce and Nanette were also very loving and giving to me and let me stay and live with them in their home in Beverly Hills. Their house had previously been lived in by Marlo Thomas and her comedian father, Danny Thomas, the founder of St. Jude's Children's Cancer Hospital in Memphis, Tennessee.

I will always appreciate my cousins Bruce and Nanette for letting me live with them for four months because UCLA Medical Center was just seven minutes away from their house. There was no way I could have commuted from Brea, California, every day for treatment, as I plainly did not have the energy to do it. Again, I am very grateful for my cousins. My brother Steve would drive down, stay with Bruce and Nanette, and visit me in the hospital every day. He was very loving and caring to me during this time.

This experience reminds me of the period of time, from ages eight to thirteen, when I was very depressed and ran away from home twenty times and felt like killing myself. My parents were calling the police to take me to juvenile hall, when immediately upon his arrival home, my nineteen-year-old brother, Steve, hung up the phone. He confronted my parents and informed them that he was taking me to Santa Barbara to live with him, and he protected me.

When I lived with my brother Steve, he made me feel very welcome and introduced me to all his friends. I felt very loved and accepted for the first time in my life. I want to say thank you, Steve, for all your love, support, and kindness. I will always be grateful to you. This shows how one person's kind act in the moment can change someone else's entire life forever.

My cancer treatment was an extremely hard experience. Unless a person has gone through a series of treatments and surgery, he or she can have no idea what it is like. If the cancer does not kill you, the treatment can. This was the hardest time of my life. I really suffered and was very sick for a long time. After three neck surgeries, three months of radiation, and two months of chemotherapy, it took me two years to fully recover. I lost two years of my life and had to retire from my successful career as a salesman.

However, I had a lot of friends to talk with on the phone during my treatments, and they really helped me get through it. Having friends was very important to me. They provided love and support and were just there for me. I had one very good friend who I would talk to from New Jersey named Ken Luehman. He was very supportive and encouraging to me. He told me over the phone one night, "I am going to tell you something very important that I don't want you to forget." He told me, and I quote, "Adversity makes greatness."

I wrote that down on a three-by-five-inch index card and kept it in my wallet the whole time I was getting cancer treatments. These words were very powerful to me. I will never forget them. They gave me the strength and energy to deal with my cancer. Remember, words can be very powerful symbols to have a good attitude. My attitude was very positive throughout, and that helped me greatly during my treatments. I am very grateful to you, Ken Luehman.

I came back home to Brea, California, in September 1999. I will never forget when I visited my daughter Sarah at her elementary school. She was nine years old and in fourth grade. She saw me on the field of her school, and we ran to each other. We were both crying tears of joy, and we hugged very, very tightly. Sarah said, "I missed you, Daddy, and I love you." That was a very beautiful moment that I will never forget.

Thank you, Sarah, for that profound moment in my life. I was so happy to see you. I love you. That moment was one of the happiest times in my life.

After the cancer treatments, I got stronger and stronger. I went back to UCLA every six months for checkups, chest X-rays, and radiation checks. I joined four cancer support groups at different Southern California hospitals, which really helped me.

I will never forget what my doctor said when I came into his office for my twentieth visit: "What the hell are you doing here? Why did you come to see me?"

I said, "You told me to see you every six months."

He said, "Oh, I did? Huh!" Then he said, "Marty, I only take care of sick patients, and I don't take care of well patients like you. I am discharging you today, and I never want to see you ever again." That is the best news to hear from your doctor, from that bedside manner point of view.

Then I went to see my radiation oncologist, and he said, "Marty, you are cured."

I then said, "You UCLA doctors have saved my life two times."

The social worker, Pam, who had been so sweet and kind and caring to me over the years, said, "I know we saved your life once, but how did we save your life twice?"

I told her that thirty-seven years earlier I had gone to UCLA for counseling because I was a very sad and depressed twelve-year-old boy, and the counselor helped me to build confidence, self-esteem, self-love.

She said, "Marty, what was the name of the counselor?"

I said, "Dr. James Q. Simmons."

She said, "Oh my God! That doctor retired a few years ago as the CEO of the UCLA hospital. He was the best counselor in the whole world. He got to the very top of this profession."

I'd had the best person to guide me back to life. The wisdom here is that if you want something in your life, you need to ask for it. If you do not ask for things, you get nothing. In very important crossroad moments in my life, I would ask my dad for help, and I always got the help I needed.

Cancer was my best and greatest teacher. Because I believe when I got cancer, I did not say, "Why me?" I said, "Why not me!" Cancer was my greatest teacher because before cancer, I thought everything was about me. I was very selfish, narcissistic, self-absorbed, and self-centered. Living in boarding schools had made me grow up very quickly. I'd had to become more like an adult to survive.

During my second major surgery at UCLA Medical Center, I had the defining moment in my life. I had an epiphany, a transformation if you will. I had seventy stitches and seventy staples in my neck and shoulder. When I came out of the recovery room and went to my own room and was in my hospital bed for two weeks, I had an unbelievable moment.

My brother Steve was visiting me from Santa Barbara. I thought to myself that I must change from being an egotistical jerk to a loving, kind, giving, and caring human being. I then said aloud to Steve, "Steve, I want to get closer to you. Please tell me your true feelings."

At that point and moment in time, I completely surrendered my ego to be totally vulnerable. I shed my skin to become humble and free to be nice to people. At that incredible moment, I knew my purpose in life was to be kind to people and to be in service to others. I totally got outside myself with the intention to be compassionate and spread love to myself and others. I felt at total peace with myself at that amazing time of transformation.

After cancer, I became more loving, giving, and caring of others. I learned that it was not all about me; it is about everyone. I learned compassion. Cancer taught me to give back to others and to serve others. Cancer told me the purpose of my life. This was a very defining point in my life: What is the purpose of life? Why am I here? What is the meaning of my life?

Again, my greatest purpose is to serve others. But I take it one step further: service to others with no expectations. The wisdom here is if you do not expect things in your life, then you will not be disappointed. Cancer also taught me to have courage and be strong and that I could overcome anything. Remember, courage is the greatest quality of a warrior. I got a tremendous amount of courage when I was very sick and could have died.

Today, I am a three-time cancer survivor; I had throat cancer and then skin cancer before, and now I have prostate cancer. I was most recently advised to have prostate surgery, chemotherapy, and radiation. Instead, I choose to extend my life by following a holistic integrative healing path.

I changed my diet, and I am now a vegan. I stay positive, attend positive classes, read positive books, listen to wonderful music, and love my family and soul mate. Life is about having fun all the time. I am under physician's care and monitor my Prostate Specific Antigen (PSA) every six months to one year. My PSA is stable at this time. I want also to note that I am a miracle. Yes, I believe in miracles. If you believe, you will receive.

Again, the wisdom here is as follows:

1. *Ask* for any help you need from your higher power and/or your angels.
2. *Believe* you are going to get that help you need.
3. *Receive* the help you need.
4. Then *take action!*

You have to do these four things or nothing will happen for you in your life; this is my belief system. My hope here is that you believe in miracles and make the best life possible for each and every person. Thank you all!

When I finished my cancer treatment at UCLA Medical Center in Los Angeles, California in September, 1999, I had my last test which was a Magnetic Resonance Imaging (MRI). I was in a casket-like chamber for 2-3 hours. I was told not to move while the doctor played loud drumming music. I felt very claustrophobic and scared. This was the last hurtle I had to overcome. The next week I went back for my results.

The doctor came into the examination room and said, "I have the best possible news for you. You have no cancer anywhere in your body!" It doesn't get any better than that. I was cancer-free with tests that proved it.

To celebrate this final victory, that day I attended a celebrity professional tennis match at UCLA Tennis Center. My front row seat nearly put me on the court with Pete Sampras and Andre Agassi, the two top ranking tennis players worldwide. They played doubles with Robin Williams and Billie Crystal, two of the best comedians in the world.

I had the time of my life watching them and feeling the greatest relief ever, knowing I had beaten cancer. Sports and cancer saved my life once again. I'm grateful and I live in gratitude every single day of this life.

I'm a living miracle. Bless you all!

I had another recent experience with an ear, nose, and throat doctor. My voice had become raspy and hoarse, so she put two or three scopes with cameras down my throat to see what was there. With my three-time cancer history, I always get concerned when doctors examine me.

To my relief, she said I was fine; there were no polyps or tumors and my throat was clear. I then said to the doctor, "Why is my voice always hoarse?"

She answered, "I have the answer. Mr. Cole, you talk too much. You never stop talking. Why don't you be quiet?"

I asked her, "Is there any other reason why I might be having this condition?"

The doctor said again, "I have the answer. Mr. Cole, you are just old. That's your problem."

We know some doctors can be very blunt and don't have a good bedside manner or behaviors. My point here is, if you don't like the doctor or you don't feel comfortable with what he or she is telling you, you should leave the office immediately and get a second or even a third opinion. Doctors do not know everything; that is why they call their profession a "practice." Plus, a lot of doctors do not do any research on your condition, illness, or disease.

I recommend that if you have a serious medical problem, go to the doctor and hospital that does research. This could save your life just as it saved mine at UCLA Medical Center eighteen years ago. I am very grateful that my family got a second opinion, and that is why I love life today and am alive today.

About seven or eight years after I got my cancer in my tonsils, I learned where the cancer had come from: the human papillomavirus (HPV)! At a lecture I attended at the University of California at Irvine Medical Center in Orange, California, the chief head and neck surgeon said the research showed that there is a 97 percent chance I got my cancer from having oral sex with women. I was shocked by these findings because I had never been told how I got cancer. I was a forty-five-year-old man who did not smoke and drank alcohol only socially. At the time of my treatment, my UCLA doctors had said they were baffled and had no idea how I got cancer. I am in the medical books as the youngest person to get this kind of cancer. It is not an award I cherish, but I am grateful that cancer changed my life for the better.

I also learned from the UCI doctors that everyone has cancer cells in his or her body. Our immune systems kill 90 percent of all cancer cells just through our natural defense system. However, 10 percent of the time, our immune systems are weakened by illness and not taking care of ourselves. Then and only then will the cancer cells take over and the person develop cancer. The doctors said my cancer could have been growing for twenty years before diagnosis.

What I learned from all of this is that I forgive myself and others for getting cancer. I do not cast blame or complain about what happened to me. Everything happens for a reason and for my benefit, no matter what it is. The wisdom here is to be careful in your lifestyle. We all need to make good choices on our journeys of life.

Finally, here is an extremely important piece of advice I want to give to parents, grandparents, and all teenagers out there in the world: please get your loved ones vaccinated with the HPV shots to prevent them from contracting the virus. The Centers for Disease Control and Prevention recommend vaccination for all preteen boys and girls at age 11 or 12 so they are protected before ever being exposed to the virus. This is paramount to protect future generations from getting cancer of the head and neck areas of the body.

Chapter 5

Meeting a Spiritual Angel Who Guided My Life

I met Frankie in 2003 at the Krikorian Theater in the Los Angeles area. It was a beautiful first time to meet this very special woman. I could tell the very first moment I met her that she was an angel from God. Frankie was warm, friendly, and bubbly and a very spiritual soul. I got to know her during the two and a half years that she flew into my life.

This woman was the most spiritual person I have ever known. She was so advanced down the path of life. I learned more from her than from anyone in my entire life. She taught me metaphysics and quantum New Age philosophies. She told me about the Institute of Noetic Sciences (IONS), which was founded by Dr. Edgar Mitchell. Dr. Mitchell was one of only twelve men who walked on the moon as part of the Apollo 14 space mission in 1971.

I learned from her about meditation, Reiki, yoga, wisdom circles, drum circles, sound healing, crystal singing bowls, mediumship/clairvoyance, psychic exploration, UFOs, holistic healing techniques, the Church of Religious Science, the mind, the body, the spirit, and the soul connections. Frankie was very smart and had an extreme amount of wisdom, more than any person I have ever met. We went to see many healers in different areas of life. The healing meditation was very interesting to me.

One area that was the most profound to me was called tantra, which combines spirituality and sexuality as one. This was the most powerful experience I've ever had. Tantra developed in India more than three thousand years ago. It is about truly loving your partner and honoring the person (you and your partner) with truth and pure love for each other. It involves really thinking about the other person first before you think of yourself. It is being in alignment with all of your chakras, your seven energy centers in your body.

There are seven chakra energy centers in the body, and each has its own meaning:

1. *Root Chakra*—"I am." The root chakra is at the base of your spine or tailbone. It represents being

grounded in the body, our humanity, elimination, and survival. Exhale *"lum."*

2. *Sacral Chakra*—"I feel." The sacral chakra is in the sexual organs. It symbolizes creativity. Exhale *"vum."*

3. *Solar Plexus Chakra*—"I do." That is the gut of feelings. It represents our mastery of self in the world. Exhale *"rum."*

4. *Heart Chakra*—"I love." The center of the body, the heart. I believe this is the most important chakra. The wisdom here is to follow your heart. It represents love and compassion. Exhale *"yum."*

5. *Throat Chakra*—"I speak." In the neck, the vocal cords. This is the chakra of power. Exhale *"hum."*

6. *Third Eye Chakra*—"I see." Above the eyebrows. It represents the intuition of your thoughts, feelings, and emotions, a union with God. Exhale *"shum."*

7. *Crown Chakra*—"I understand." On the top of the head. Be open to the enlightenment of the universe. Exhale *"om."*

Just remember, the chakras play a very important role in the energy centers in the body. Use them to gain awareness, consciousness, and mindfulness in your life. Practice these chants by breathing energy into each chakra and then saying the words listed as you exhale.

Frankie taught me so many insights into the power of the heart. She became my soul mate, lover, best friend, mentor, coach, teacher, and the most influential person in my life. She went on to become a tantra teacher and spiritual master. When she flew away from me, it broke my heart for a very long time.

The most important lesson I learned from Frankie occurred the day she said, "I think you should start a Wisdom Circle."

I said, "What is a Wisdom Circle?" I had no idea.

She said, "It is a group of people you form to encourage, inspire, motivate, and give love and kindness."

I said, "No. No way!" But she never took no for an answer.

I started the Wisdom Circle in September 2005. It was a community group, and I became the community leader. I started with two people and at its peak it grew to fifty-four. At first I had it at my house, which we pretty much outgrew. The parent organization of the Wisdom Circle was the Institute of Noetic Sciences (IONS), founded by astronaut Dr. Edgar D. Mitchell, who I mentioned earlier .

I got to know Dr. Mitchell personally. I would go to conventions, lectures, and seminars where he would discuss the collective consciousness of the world. He talked about having awareness of yourself and everything around you. He would say, "Energy is everything" and "everything is energy." We are energy sources with amazing abilities. He would also always say, "Be open to the possibilities."

I met him five or six times. The most profound experience

I had with him was in July 2011 in San Francisco, California, at an IONS conference. Dr. Mitchell and I, just the two of us, talked alone for thirty minutes at a cocktail party for IONS community group leaders.

He told me he had just gotten off the phone with one of the IONS community leaders in Pakistan, who said terrorist groups were radicalizing and hiring massive numbers of suicide bombers to kill Americans and Europeans. He told me to my face, and I quote, "Marty, go back to Orange County, California, to your Wisdom Circle, and spread more love to this world." It does not get any more powerful than that!

Dr. Mitchell always told me, "Love is the most important thing."

He also told me that we need to have much more cooperation between the people of this world. Cooperation is the key, he said, if the planet is going to survive. Former President Barack Obama said the same thing about the need for cooperation in his final press conference.

We lost Dr. Mitchell in February 2016 at the age of eighty-five. He was my teacher, coach, mentor, and friend, and we both have the same birthday—September 17. He truly was a pioneer of the human spirit, an innovator, and a free spirit. He was a very open-minded and gifted leader.

He touched my life in so many ways. When he passed away, I was taking a shower. I felt his spirit enter my body.

I kid you not! This was a very emotional and profound experience. He will live within me forever. The power of his spirit lives in my heart. Never underestimate the power of the heart. I listen to my heart. It is my guiding light of wisdom.

Chapter 6

The Wisdom Healing Circle

Our community group had two names. First, it was called the Wisdom Circle, and later it was called the Wisdom Healing Circle. We were a very interesting group of people that included teachers, artists, musicians, and both spiritually aware and spiritually unaware people.

As the community group grew over ten years, we hosted some very diverse guest speakers that talked to us on a wide range of subjects over the years, including meditation, yoga, laughter yoga, Reiki, animal communications, drum circles, crystal singing bowls circle, holistic percussion, numerology, mindfulness, gratitude, love, relationships, sound healing, music concerts, positive attitudes, social psychology, past life regression, HeartMath, holistic medicine, herbs, healthy eating, homeless people, homeless shelters, channeling the spirit world, artist showcases, hula dancing, ancestors.com, chanting circles, the power of silent meditation, the power of prayer, wisdom healing, Pranic Healing, The Power of Healing Stones, What Are You Grateful For?, *The Power of Now, The Four Agreements, Rhinoceros Success, The Motivation Manifesto, How to Heal Your Life, Heart Thoughts, Rich Dad, Poor Dad, A Course in Miracles, Excuses Be Gone,* and *The HeartMath Solution.*

The glue that held our group together was the people. We had thirty regular attendees on average. I think the most popular night was poetry night, when thirty people would get up in front of a microphone and read the poems they had written. Also, a very popular Wisdom Healing Circle was *A Course in Miracles.* In the ten years of the Wisdom Healing Circle, we had more than three hundred people come and go to meetings.

I would like to acknowledge three people who passed away during the time we held the Wisdom Healing Circle. The first person is Esther Rabinowitz, the queen of wisdom. She was the most giving and loving person. If there were twenty-five people at the meeting, she would bring a potluck dinner big enough to serve one hundred people. The second person is Phil Kaus, a very sweet and very funny man. I met Phil at the cancer support group at the University of California of Irvine. Phil was nice and giving to everyone around him. The third person is Carol White, a beautiful soul. I met Carol at her own Wisdom

Circle in Fountain Valley, California. She was a professional clown and the funniest person I have ever met. She gave me inspiration and wisdom and cared about people very deeply. All three of these beautiful souls will live in our hearts and memories forever.

The biggest thing I learned in the Wisdom Healing Circle is this: I talked earlier in this book about Dr. Wayne Dyer's beliefs. He was a great teacher to me and wrote the book that our group studied called *Excuses Be Gone*. His frequent teachings were, "What people say gets in your way", "Every action we have is a choice", and "Our life is all about choices." The wisdom here is that all things are possible. I can do anything in my life because there is a spiritual solution for every problem. "The average person has fifteen excuses not to do anything," Wayne said. "All excuses are a misalignment." Wayne Dyer also said this very important passage at an "I Can Do It" speaking event in Pasadena, California, one of his last lectures: "We are all infinite spiritual beings having a temporary human experience. Find that within yourself."

Albert Einstein once said, "Know our source and think like God thinks." All that we are is from our thoughts. "Move away from excuses," Dyer said, because awareness and ego cannot exist together. Ego means "edging God out." We need to think from the highest places that exist. People are living in fear, worry, and anger. My definition of fear is "false events and/or evidence appearing real."

We need to move away from this by letting go and letting God! Let go of all things that do not serve you. What I learned the most is to take action in your life so that you can create the best life for yourself. Wayne would always say, "When you change the things you look at in your life, your life changes. We all have a choice every day," as well as, "Do I want to live with love or do I want to live in fear?" This is from *A Course in Miracles*.

Or as the Dalai Lama says of love, "The planet does not need more successful people. The planet desperately needs more peacemakers, healers, restorers, storytellers, and lovers of all kinds."

Going to see the Dalai Lama live and in person really inspires me. I have seen the fourteenth His Holiness in the flesh five times. Each time I have been amazed by his presence. He says that compassion, love, and kindness are the most important things for yourself and others. We need to inspire and empower people in our lives, here and around the world. We all want to live in peace. We are all human brothers and sisters. Then he says, laughing, "I am very happy right now!"

Let us strive for motivation and leadership. He says he feels people's energy and that it is okay if you are not into religion as long as you carry the message of love and compassion to others. The real message of God is the passion we are seeking here. In our lives, we have too much of these negative emotions:

- stress
- loneliness
- depression
- worry

The problem we face is that we worry too much. We ourselves are creating all the problems we have. The problems are interconnected in that we have too much emotion and anger, and we cannot see the reality of life. We all need to develop a calm mind. Drugs and/or alcohol will make this worse. People must work toward positive emotions. We do that by having more wisdom. People who are full of fear start hating other people and therefore cannot have a calm mind.

The Dalai Lama says we need more cooperation. Does that sound like a familiar theme throughout my book? He also says we must develop more friendship, trust, and warm-heartedness toward others. I am asking you all to please have more compassionate hearts and spread love to yourself and others. I hope we all practice forgiveness, tolerance, and love. And we need to continue to pray, study science, respect all people with nonviolence and harmony, and promote more common sense.

Life is about having fun. Please have fun, more fun, and the most fun. Please give more love to your family and friends. Give more love and attention to your children. Family is the most important thing.

Of all the wisdom I have learned in my life, the common

theme that keeps getting my attention is it is all about how you treat people.

When I listened to Colin Powell, a former U.S. Secretary of State and former Joint Chief of Staff, at an Anaheim success conference, he said we should be nicer to people, whether they are garbage collectors, parking attendants, or waiters. When he was in Washington DC, he would always treat the parking garage people with the utmost respect because they were getting him the best parking spot or getting his car for him. He says to do this in all areas of life, both at work and in relationships with people. We are all the same. We are no better than anyone else, and no one is better than us.

I have learned that wisdom is experience and experience is wisdom. Many people today are living in fear, worry, anxiety, and hatred. We must live in love, not fear. Be fearless. Do not be afraid. We cannot lead ourselves and others without trust. "Trust is a must!" A friend of mine named Sandy Freud always says that.

There is too much fear in the world today. Just look on social media and or watch the news. People are saying, "What is going to happen to me in this country or the world? Am I going to get deported? Is my freedom going to be taken away?" Many people are freaking out and living in fear. Do you remember what *fear* stands for? False events or evidence appearing real. The problem with a lot of people is that they are living in the past or worrying about what is going to happen in the future. That is not living or enjoying life.

We need to live in the present. Eckhart Tolle calls it "the power of now." That is why it is called the present. It is a gift that keeps giving, right here, right now. All that matters is that we choose to live right now, in this present moment. If people do not learn this, they will suffer greatly. If we choose to live in the past, we will be depressed. If we live in the future, then we will have anxiety. Why do some people choose to suffer? Every day we have a choice: we can live with love or we can live with fear. Everything in life is a choice! I hope we choose to live in the present.

I believe today that spirituality is the most important topic people want to know about. Spirituality is not the same as religion. Religion and politics are real turnoffs for me. They start so many wars and have caused the deaths of so many people.

Spirituality, on the other hand, is very important. It includes the laws of the universe, the Law of Attraction. The Law of Attraction works like this: If you know who you are and you know what you want, then you attract what you want. However, if you do not know who you are and do not know what you want, then you attract what you do not want. This is so true in relationships with people, places, and things.

There are three important questions in our lives:

- What is my purpose?
- Why am I here?
- What is life all about?

We all must have a purpose in life. The purpose of my life is to be in service to others and expect nothing. If I expect nothing, I do not get disappointed. The wisdom here is that we must find meaning in our lives. Then we can be happy and feel good.

My forever friend, Fred Afshar, shared this Persian saying:

> *Think good.*
> *Talk good.*
> *Do good.*

And, I would add, feel good!

I've learned over the years that we must strive for more self-love for ourselves! Just like Whitney Houston sings in her song "The Greatest Love of All," that greatest love is learning to love yourself. If you have trouble with loving yourself, I recommend standing in front of the mirror every day and saying, "I love myself! I'm awesome, and I rock!" My soul mate, Frankie, taught me another good technique: put your arms around yourself and say, "I love that inner child in you." Another good gift you can give yourself is to act childlike, not childish. Keep the child alive within yourself and you will have much more fun in life. Make fun a priority!

We must learn to be good navigators in our lives. If we do not, we will be eaten by all the alligators. Please do not take that literally. It is just a saying I made up. I feel that we need to keep going to the light like the symbol of the lighthouse. Light is healing, and healing is light. When we are in darkness, we lose our way and get lost.

I have learned that energy is everything and everything is energy. I believe we are all healers. We have 30 watts of electricity in our bodies 24-7. We have the ability to heal ourselves just by believing that we can do so. We have all heard the saying, "mind over matter!"

If we have an illness, I believe we should not give that sickness energy by worrying about it. I think we can get better naturally. We can heal ourselves by having a very positive attitude. If we practice gratitude, I believe our lives will improve greatly. Remember, we are our thoughts, feelings, and emotions. We have the power to change it, fix it, and control it if we believe we can!

I believe we need to walk and go into nature. When we are in nature, we become more balanced and more grounded. Animals, trees, and flowers are our teachers. They live in the present and do not judge us. They just give us unconditional love.

The wisdom here is that I hope we learn this, because many people do not live in the moment, as well as judge others and give only conditional love. I feel that judgment and lack of acceptance is not love. It comes from ego and fear only.

We all need to work to

- stop judging people;
- live in the present;
- let go of the past;
- not worry about the future; and
- give unconditional love.

In addition, I recommend that everyone go hug a tree. The tree is an energy source and gives off electrons. When I hug a tree for ten minutes, my whole body starts vibrating with energy. You might want to do it in private, because some people might think you are weird. Since we're on the subject of vibrating energy, I totally believe in sound healing, which is promoted by any sound that creates vibrational energy movement: singing, humming, chanting, laughing, and listening to your favorite music. There is scientific evidence showing that sound can heal your body at the cellular level.

At a concert called "Holistic Sound Healing" with Mike Garson, a former keyboardist for David Bowie who was conducting the big band, I saw a female dancer who had full-blown Parkinson's Disease and could only walk with a walker. When the band played the Brazilian tango, this woman got up and danced a full ten-minute tango with her husband with no problem. After that, she fell back into her walker chair. I have never seen anything like it, and her husband and doctors could not explain it. The power of sound healing is proven to help heal your body and create well-being.

At a 2013 four-day retreat in Cancun, Mexico, with Esther Hicks, the beautiful soul who helped educate us on the Law of Attraction, I learned to focus on the things that please me. We all make choices every day. We all need to do a better job of expressing ourselves, who we really are, and choosing *for* our highest good.

The wisdom I learned is that we need to never stop asking ourselves these two questions:

1. What do I want?
2. And what do I need?

The more we are attuned to life and feel alive, the less sleep we will need. Positive momentum is increased by meditation. Meditation is just sitting in a private place for ten to thirty minutes, preferably with your eyes closed, and saying a mantra. The mantra is made up of three symbol words (e.g., "do, re, mi" or "la de da"). Keep saying the mantra over and over until your mind is calm and clear. It is best to try not to have thoughts. If they come, repeat the mantra again and again. When you practice meditation, you are really helping to heal your mind, body, spirit, and soul. I just gave you a priceless course in meditation that I learned from the Beatles' guru, the Maharishi Yogi.

Don't forget that deep breathing is the most important thing before, during, and after meditation.

The Wisdom Healing Circle taught me the power of gratitude. Do not ever underestimate it. When we practice being thankful on a regular basis, I believe more blessings and miracles will come our way. I am living proof of it. It works for me big time in my life.

The more we go with the flow and keep a positive attitude of gratitude, the better. We manifest our affirmations. We can do anything we want just by our thoughts, feelings, and emotions. When I have made good choices, better things come to me all the time. Miracles happen for me on a regular basis.

If we can create balance and stay grounded, we can have more vibrational movement, which will result in energies flowing and healing our bodies. To stay grounded, we must do three important things, according to Scott Alexander:

1. Have freedom
2. Have fun
3. Have adventure and act like a teenager

The Rhino man told me this himself in person over a three-hour lunch on December 2, 2015.

Remember what our teachers are saying. Teachers are very important, and we need to listen and respect them. Teachers say that communication and relationships are the keys to a happy life. The lesson here is that we should keep the spark alive and keep watering the garden of our relationships. Please try not to make excuses and be lazy with others. Keep the momentum going and stay in the vortex. When we are happy, the momentum gets greater and greater and our lives become more powerful.

Being sensitive to how you feel is what matters here. People who are not accepting of where they are in their lives are the ones who are not happy. The wisdom here is to accept yourself and others and try not to judge people. When we are in judgment, we are coming from ego and fear. Remember that everything is about love and love is everything.

Most people are afraid to use their freedom. Use your freedom or lose your freedom. More and more people are living in fear today. They are afraid of what is going to happen to them now and in the future.

My advice is to stop worrying about the future. It is not even here yet. Live in the present moment. Also, get out of your past; you will only be depressed. And again, stop the fear of tomorrow or you will continue to have anxiety and more stress, anger, and frustration. Instead, think of something you love and are grateful for.

I will continue to say gratitude is the best attitude. The better the attitude, the more the gratitude. When you are in a tough situation, I recommend that you say, "Let go, let God" (or your higher power or belief system). We need to feel worthy. Only then we will feel whole and complete within ourselves.

One of my teachers is Bruce Lipton. Well, we are each other's teachers. I met Bruce in Tucson in 2009 at an IONS convention. Bruce Lipton is a microbiologist who liked to talk and write only about science. We talked at length face-to-face. I recommended that, in teaching metaphysics, he needed to incorporate love into his lectures and books. He listened to me and then wrote the book *Creating Heaven on Earth—The Honeymoon Effect*.

At Bruce's workshop at the Institute of Noetic Sciences conference in Indian Wells, California, in July 2013, he said that 80 percent of what we are told as children are negative things. Bruce urged us to stop believing in those lies and change right now. We are totally worthy just the way we are.

He told me, "Marty, I remember you from Tucson, where you told me we need to spread more love in our lectures and books. Marty, you are my teacher." After Bruce said that to me, I went outside with my soul mate and cried tears of joy for thirty minutes. Remember, we all are each other's students and teachers.

Let me explain some more that it is all energy and the more vibrational harmony we can have in our lives, the better. Again, energy is everything and everything is energy in this world and universe. That is why we hear a chirp from space. NASA put a listening satellite device deep in space, and we hear a chirp, like a bird makes, signaling back to Earth. The universe is talking and communicating with us.

People ask me all the time what they should do in their lives. I say to them, "Follow your heart, not your head." People appreciate me saying that. I always have the same answer for anyone who asks.

Let us just practice pure joy and pure love and not fight for our desires. Be free and have an open mind and spirit to keep your energy flowing. I believe you will live a longer life if you do not make it hard on yourself and instead just accept yourself the way you are. Remember, we are not ordinary; we are extraordinary. Make your life simple, not complicated. Just love yourself as you really are. The love, courage, and wisdom here is that your choices create the people, places, and things you attract in your life.

Another important point here is to listen and write down your dreams, whether they are conscious or unconscious. Your dreams are your teacher. They are telling you who you really are. The better you feel about yourself, the better your dreams will guide you to understand your life with more awareness. Be playful and childlike in your life and you will have a lot more fun, joy, love, peace, and most importantly, happiness.

I am a light worker, shining my light just like a lighthouse. Just remember, light is healing and healing is light. This is why I love lighthouses. I use my third eye, my intuition, as a guiding beacon of light. I shine it like a spotlight and rotate it **360** degrees to other people. I am a light source of healing white light energy, an ocean of white light energy, if you will.

I hope you do not waste your time and energy on negative things and darkness. I do not like to go to the dark side of life myself. I am an optimist, not a pessimist. To me the glass is half-full, not half-empty. I do not believe, as some people do, in thinking of the worst-case scenarios in most situations. I feel that focusing on the worst-cases scenario, as many people and organizations automatically do, causes more fear and worry and detracts from the positive momentum that creates success. Ninety percent of the things we worry about and fear never happen. Worrying is a total waste of your time and energy! How's that working for you?

Remember, there is a spiritual answer for every problem. So let it be and so it is. Everything works out for us! Everything happens for our benefit. So just love life and love yourself and be grateful for everything. Now that I've got your attention, my hope is that you will not buy into the fear that is out there in our country and throughout the world.

This is a letter I wrote on September 18, 2007, on how I was feeling about our Wisdom Circle:

> It is a beautiful day today, and I thank God for everything in my life. I thank you, God, for our Wisdom Circle and all the loving, caring,

and kind people who come and share their thoughts, feelings, emotions, and experiences with our community. I am very grateful for everything in my life every day. I am very happy for all the things I have, not what I do not have.

I believe in the Law of Attraction, which is one of the laws of the universe that responds when you go for what you want in your life by taking action and having the courage to make things happen. I also believe in helping people by serving people and doing good deeds for people on a daily basis and not wanting anything in return. This is the purpose of my journey. Life is not a destination; it is the journey. Thank you, God, for everything in every way and every day.

Love and blessings,
Marty Cole.

This letter is exactly what the Wisdom Circle was. Let me explain what I mean by this.

Every year for nine years in a row, I would take twenty to thirty people to the Fullerton, California, homeless shelter. We would pass out three hundred food gift cards, one for each homeless person. The people living there would tell stories of how they could not get jobs because the address they put on job applications was the address of the homeless shelter. The employer would not hire them because they were homeless.

What really stood out for me with this experience was that many of the homeless people had better attitudes and were more grateful than many millionaires I know. Some people who have a lot of money like to complain, blame, and explain their problems. Some of these folks are not happy or grateful.

One year I met a homeless woman named Ileen, who I met when I was giving out Christmas gift cards at the shelter. She became an author and wrote a book for homeless people on how to get out of being homeless. She wrote a self-help book on believing in a higher power and being grateful for your life and that you are still alive. I read her story in the student Titan newspaper at Cal State University Fullerton.

A story like this is very touching and moving. That is why I practice gratitude and want to give back and help people and expect nothing in return. The wisdom here is to be in service to others, and again, that is what I believe is the purpose of our lives. It gives you meaning when you are being loving and compassionate to others, especially the less fortunate.

I believe to make these things work we need to take the following actions:

- Find our inner wisdom
- Find our passion
- Change ourselves and the world
- Ask ourselves, "What is the purpose of my life?"
- Serve others to make humankind better

What a powerful experience it was being a community group leader under the direction of Dr. Edgar Mitchell. He founded IONS more than forty-four years ago because he had a profound experience as an astronaut on the Apollo 14 flight to the moon. After he walked the moon, as he walked up the ladder to the lunar module, he had an epiphany. He looked at the magnificent colors of the Earth and how beautiful the living breathing ecosystem of a planet looked. He said to himself, "When I go back to Earth, I want to start an organization to save the planet." As you know now, he was successful.

Dr. Mitchell also related that while on the moon, he saw how perfect Earth is. He knew that some force greater than mankind, greater than even our solar system, must have created life and our universe.

The theme of my first IONS conference, held June 16–19, 2009, in Tucson, Arizona, was "Toward a Global Shift: Seeing the Field of Collective Change." I learned there that we need to be living the future now. What that meant to me was that we need to work with nature and learn from nature. That means communicating with the forces of nature. We need to be in the silence of nature and feel oneness with nature and wildlife. When we do this, we can be in balance and harmony and be more grounded in our lives.

Find ways to experience more of life. For example, when you get to a fork in the road, take the road less traveled. We need to have more awareness and be mindful.

Mindfulness means living in the present moment, right now, without judgment. When you do this, you will have more light, joy, peace, and love in your life. Remember, the universe supports those who support the universe. What is very important here is to make a shift in your life. A shift means changing yourself from dying to being born. When we change ourselves, we change the world at the same time. If we turn within, we can find a higher purpose and develop a successful way of communicating that purpose to others.

I think if we create a more positive community, we will have better relationships with family and friends at home, school, and work. We are all connected, and our DNA is 99 percent the same. If we can do this, we will bring more peace and harmony and love to this planet. By practicing these principles, we can have more healing in our lives. If we have the right relationships, we will move toward a unity of people here and around the world.

To do this, there are four things we need to be aware of:

- Be open to becoming a spiritual warrior.
- Be open to building a new world.
- Be open to finding your true being.
- Be open to the universe.

The second IONS conference I attended was July 20–24, 2011, in San Francisco. The theme was "Tools and Technologies: For a World Transforming." There I learned that we need to transform ourselves. We do this through a shift in consciousness or, in more simple terms, by having more awareness of our inner selves. If we look at people with unloving eyes, it is uncomfortable, stressful, and unfriendly. If we look at people with loving eyes, we are looking with more compassion, love, gratitude, and friendliness. I recommend that we smile more at the people around us.

We all have choices in everything we do. We can come from love or fear. Each person can only control what he or she is doing; we cannot control others or their behaviors . Again, the wisdom is live in the moment, right here, right now. It is called "The Power of Now." We need to see things differently and try to see things from the other person's point of view. Instead of getting angry at another person, we need to see life with different eyes and be more compassionate and friendly and more comfortable with the person.

I recommend making affirmations for yourself. Affirmations will help you work with your mind and create a balance within your body, soul, and spirit. An example of an affirmation is, "I am whole and complete just as I am. I am worthy and I am good enough." We need to learn from the inside out and follow our hearts!

Here are the five things I learned from my second IONS conference:

- Make positive affirmations.
- Make positive manifestations.
- Wisdom is power with thoughts, feelings, and emotions.
- Communicate in a peaceful, loving, non-threatening way.
- Support others in your community.

Another very, very important field of study is called HeartMath. I was not even supposed to take this class at the IONS conference. I signed up for a meditation class and then my heart said, "No, not another meditation class." I went to the front desk and asked if any other class was open. The IONS staff recommended the HeartMath class, and there was only one ticket left. Remember, everything that happens is for our benefit.

When I entered this class late, the teacher asked, "Why are you late?" I explained and then the teacher said, "Why are you taking the class?" I said I was following my heart. The teacher said, "Perfect answer. You were meant to take this class."

I learned from the HeartMath philosophy to open my

heart to restore love and care for other people. The most important thing in our lives is universal love, which means being in the right relationship with ourselves. When you come from love, you will have full and complete healing. When we have compassion and caring for ourselves and others, we will find inner truth, beauty, and what it means to be truly human. HeartMath taught me that we have a small brain in our hearts that has thoughts, feelings, and emotions. That is why we need to follow our hearts. Never underestimate the power of the heart.

According to research, our heart beats 100,000 times a day. This equals 40,000 neuron pulses per day. When our hearts and brains are aligned, we can make changes in our lives for our benefit. If they are not aligned, we make bad choices and pay the consequences; as a result, we suffer.

Again, my wisdom here is follow your heart. Let it be your guide, navigation system, and your shining light. If we can learn more balance and harmony in the heart, we can gain more wisdom to deal with stress in our lives. I believe if we live in gratitude and appreciation of things in our lives, our minds, bodies, souls, and spirits will be stronger and our immune systems will be healthy and operate on a higher functioning level.

Also, if we can work on being less judgmental of people, we will be able to reduce our stress and unhappiness. What is important here is to practice forgiveness for yourself and for others. That will definitely give you peace of mind, and following your heart will alleviate challenges in your life. The heart is the center of our bodies, and we are all healers of ourselves if we believe that we are. If we practice these ideas, we really can become healers and heal our bodies at the cellular level.

A very amazing experience happened to me when I returned home from the conference in San Francisco. The next day, a friend called me and said that there was a class at Unity of Tustin, California, that might interest me. I asked, "What is the name of the class?" My friend said, "It is called HeartMath." I never told that friend that I had just come from that class one day earlier at the IONS conference.

I called this story *synchronicity*, which means everything happens spontaneously. There are no accidents or coincidences, and everything happens for a reason and for your benefit.

I took this HeartMath class the next day and stayed with it for three straight years without missing a Tuesday night meeting. In the class, I learned to practice gratitude for each and every day. The people I got to know in this class bonded, and some of them later attended my Wisdom Circle and even my OLLI class and are today some of my closest friends.

While in the HeartMath class, I started to make affirmations to manifest the woman I wanted to meet in my life. I said over and over again that I wanted to meet a woman who was nice, sweet, gentle, kind, and tender. But at the center of my attraction, I said the woman I had not yet met must be spiritually aligned with source, mind, body, spirit, and soul connection.

I affirmed this for three months solid, and then I met my soul mate, who I named Rainbow Turtle. She became the love of my life. All the things I asked the universe for were granted to me because I believe in the Law of Attraction, which again is one of the laws of the universe. My best friend, soul mate, and life partner is the sweetest woman I have ever known.

Before I met her, I really worked on my own self-development. I visualized her to be unlike the kinds of women I had been attracted to before. The women I had been attracting before were mean, controlling, angry, gold-digging females. They were always trying to change and fix me and not accept me for who I was.

Rainbow Turtle changed everything for me in terms of being completely compatible and enjoying the same things together. Plus, she is a musician, a concert pianist. We share a mutual love for music styles of all kinds, the arts, plays, concerts, and dances. We have so many songs in our heads. The number of musicians and songs that we know is limitless. Our spiritual growth is the glue that holds us together. Our shared love of music is icing on our cake.

The next IONS conference I attended was the "Fortieth Year Celebration: Explore, Dream and Discover." It was held July 17–21, 2013, in Indian Wells, California. Dr. Jean Houston's wisdom is that we all need to be more peaceful. Just like the Dalai Lama tells us, if we have more peace within ourselves—inner peace—we will have more peace in the world. We all need to tame the ego and strive to be more humble and peaceful. It all starts and stops with being open to the possibilities of life.

These are some of the possibilities we need to focus on:

- Understanding who we are
- Empowering ourselves
- Inserting music and art back into all cultures of the world
- Controlling our anger and negative experiences
- Trying not to judge people and working on accepting each other
- Managing our time together on this Earth

Dr. Dean Radin is the chief scientist at the Institute of Noetic Sciences. Radin says the placebo effect really exists and the sugar pill works if you believe it does. Never underestimate the power of belief. If we know it is true for us, then that is all that matters. If our intention is strong, then the healing processes of our bodies begin.

Keep dreaming consciously and unconsciously, because our dreams are our teachers. Be open and aware, and then the change within you can occur.

At this IONS conference, I heard Master Mingtong Gu teach

wisdom healing qigong. He translates ancient teachings from China on healing your mind, body, spirit, and soul to create happiness. My belief system is that happiness and love is everything and everything is happiness and love. Energy is the only thing in the universe. We must use our energy to create wisdom energy. Master Gu says that we must go deeper and deeper within ourselves to find and create the changes for healing. If we keep going back to our hearts, we can start healing ourselves from disease, pain, and distress. We need to use our energies for movement, music, and visualization.

This was my journey at the conference. I felt very light on my feet with wisdom healing qigong. I have had three operations on my neck and shoulders, which led me to have a frozen neck and a frozen shoulder. Master Gu's exercises of movement enlightened my mind, body, and spirit. I was able to raise my arms for fifteen minutes. I had not been able to do that in the thirteen years since I had my surgeries. A miracle just happened for me. As you already know, I believe in miracles.

The important points I learned at this IONS convention:

> Lack of love causes disease.
> We must create a new lifestyle.
> We should practice an inner smile.
> We must love ourselves unconditionally.
> We must transform our fear to love; change
> our thoughts, feelings and emotions.

We should never give energy to fear.
Sound and vibration practices can heal.
We all have an "ocean of white light healing
energy" inside us to use and heal our lives.
The world is a circle of healing.
Sound healing energy can heal our minds
and bodies by sending messages to our inner
organs, like an internal massage.

We can all shine light to the world. That is why, again, I feel that I am a lighthouse, shining my light to others in the world like a beacon of life coming out of my third eye chakra, which is intuition.

When my soul mate Rainbow Turtle and I were having a community dinner together at the conference, a distinguished gentleman wearing a white hat and black shirt came up to us and asked if he and his friend could join us. We said they could.

It turns out he was LeVar Burton, a major television and film star. He played Kunta Kinte in the documentary *Roots* in 1977. He was also one of the stars in *Star Trek: The Next Generation*. Now on PBS, he manages and directs a children's program called *Reading Rainbow*.

He was the narrator on a PBS movie in 2012 and 2013 about the space probe Maven to the planet Mars created by the Jet Propulsion Laboratory in Pasadena, California. The chief engineer had a dream, and in his dream, he used beanbags, huge beanbags, to help with the super fast impact of the space probe when it landed on Mars. All the other missions had failed because the spacecraft had exploded on impact. NASA said it was their last chance to make an exploration of Mars happen, as it cost $2 billion. It was the first successful space probe to Mars.

The key here is that the head of the project listened to his dreams and took action. I want you all to listen to your dreams and then take action in your life. I had not yet seen his movie, and now LeVar Burton was sitting with me and telling me that it was nice having dinner with us. How sweet was that moment in time! After that, I did see the movie he narrated, and it was fantastic. I've been a *Star Trek* fan since I was thirteen!

Another person I met at this IONS conference was Don Miguel Ruiz, the author of *The Four Agreements*. The book is a very powerful wisdom to make your life more simple and easy. The four agreements are as follows:

(1) Be impeccable with your word;
(2) Don't take anything personally;
(3) Don't make assumptions;
(4) Always do your best.

I believe if we do not practice these lessons of life, we will suffer much more in our own reality.

My next IONS conference was in Oakbrook, Illinois, on July 24–26, 2015. The best part was that I got to bring my daughter Melissa, who was twenty years old at the time.

What a delight to be able to go with a beautiful young woman who was open to the possibilities of mind, body, spirit, and soul!

This wonderful adventure was made possible by a workshop I had previously attended at Sunrise—the Institute of Noetic Sciences headquarters in Petaluma, California. It is a beautiful retreat center for meditation and self-reflection in the rolling hills of Marin County near San Francisco. This earlier four-day retreat was about wisdom healing with the Master Mingtong Gu, the spiritual healer who had given me so much healing at the 2013 Indian Wells IONS conference.

The first two days of the retreat were basically a silent retreat with no talking; we were just present with ourselves. It was difficult for me for the first several hours because I am a talker. After a while, I was able to relax and let go in the silence. At the end of each night, we were guided in some chanting and sound healing. I really enjoyed the vibrational energy and felt very much at peace.

Even during our meals, we practiced mindful eating with our eyes closed, only opening our eyes for the next bite. After two days, we went into a small group of eight men only. We talked about what we had learned about ourselves from the experience. What I learned was a very profound transformation.

My daughter Melissa was a quiet young lady. She did not like to talk much. When I asked her any questions, her answers were usually one-word responses. I felt for many years that she was either ignoring me or did not like me very much. I took it personally.

Then awareness came to me at the retreat. I learned about myself and my need to accept my daughter Melissa just the way she was. If she did not talk or respond to me, it was totally okay. I just needed to love her unconditionally with no judgments. This was a huge epiphany for me to come to peace with my daughter's gift of being an introvert and loving the silence and not feeling awkward or uncomfortable.

When I came back home to Southern California, I had lunch with Melissa. I told her what I had experienced at the retreat, and I said, "If you are quiet and don't want to talk to me, I totally accept you just the way you are. I accept you with unconditional love."

My daughter replied, and I quote, "Are you serious, Dad?" She was totally shocked and surprised by my statements.

I said, "I'm very serious about what I just said."

From that moment on, my relationship with my Melissa changed 180 degrees. We became very close as a father-daughter family. The powerful wisdom I learned is to accept your family, friends, coworkers, and the people in your life just the way they are. You will have a complete shift and awareness in your relationship with others. Your world will be brighter with light. When you change with life, then the world will also change with healing energy as well. I love you, Melissa. You are my angel of my lifetime.

Now you know how my daughter and I got to the 2015 IONS convention in Oakbrook. The first words I heard there were from Deborah Jones from the Nine Gates Mystery School. Everything is vibration, and vibration is everything. We are electrical fields of vibration. (Remember, I discussed this earlier?) We have 30 watts of electricity in our bodies.

The key is that we must use the energy in our bodies to heal ourselves and the planet. An important point here is that energy flows where attention goes. We are an ocean of white light energy. We are an ocean of consciousness. The last point I want to make is that vibration is love and love is vibration. So please, spread some more love to your family, friends, coworkers, and the people you meet so that we can raise the vibration of the planet for more peace and love to the universe.

At one of these international IONS conference dinners, I was a guest speaker for 150 community group leaders from thirty countries around the world, talking about my own Wisdom Circle. The reason my Wisdom Healing Circle was the largest and longest existing group, and the most successful, is because I treated my group like my own family. I am very loving, caring, and giving to everyone. It was important to me to be generous to each and every person who came to my home. This is why my community group was very successful for ten years and served more than three hundred people who came and went during our 125 meetings. Our get-togethers were on the third Monday of each month. We inspired, moved, and touched many people, and I am very proud and grateful for that.

My daughter enjoyed the conference and connected with other young people in attendance. Melissa told me that the people there were very smart and friendly. She was open to this very new experience and told me that for the very first time, "I understand you better, Dad, and see the meaning of the group that you founded and what IONS is all about." The Institute of Noetic Sciences means living a "noetic life." The definition is "transformation and healing at the convergence of science and spirituality combined as one."

Our teacher at this conference was Dr. Marilyn Schlitz, former CEO of IONS. We learned that the power of consciousness is the power of healing ourselves. The most important thing we need to do is find purpose and meaning in life.

The three questions that came up and we were asked to answer them as part of an exercise:

- What inspires you?
- What are you afraid of?
- What gives you meaning?

The following few paragraphs explore my responses to these questions.

What gives my life meaning is learning, growing, and healing wisdom. When I experience this, I feel more connected to myself and to others. Because of it, I feel more love for myself and for others. Everything is an inside job, and my life starts and stops with my breath.

The sound healing I am teaching is making a difference with myself and my students and the wisdom healing community group. Vibrational energy is all around us if we just pay attention to it. I also believe that if we experience this peace, it will dramatically improve our immune systems and protect us from illness and disease. What I have learned from all my teachings is to believe in ourselves and to inspire people to have the courage to take action. I am not afraid of anyone or anything. I have transformed into fearlessness.

The Dalai Lama refers to this as compassion in action. Remember, our storytelling is very powerful in changing things and people, even the world. The two most important things to me in life are love and gratitude. Love is an inspired form of giving breath and life into the heart and bringing grace to the soul. Gratitude is the most important practice you can do, to be thankful for everything in your life.

The wisdom I have learned here is that we as people can get upset and depressed at any time. Then we forget everything we have learned. It goes right out the window when we are angry. My remedy here is to try not to get out of control with any anger. Take a breath and take a more peaceful approach. Look at things differently, as they say in *A Course in Miracles*. The course teaches us to come from love, not from fear. Love is the only thing that is real. Fear is an illusion. Practice love and gratitude and forgiveness on a daily basis to bring joy, happiness, and peace into your life.

The advice here is to teach as many of you, my readers, as possible to become light workers. Spread our light of love, peace, joy, and compassion to the world, one person at a time. When we do this, we "change the world and make it a better place for you and me," as Michael Jackson sings in his song "Heal the World."

I have three great questions I want you to ask yourself:

- What makes me happy today?
- Where did I experience comfort, peace, and joy today?
- Who and what inspired me today?

As Nelson Mandela of South Africa said: "Let us take care of the children. Let us take care of the seniors. Let us take care of everyone in between. Give gratitude every day. Take a life-affirming action every day, no matter how big or small. And do acts of kindness on a regular basis. Throw kindness around like a rainbow of confetti. It is the little things we do that make all the difference." Lady Gaga says, "Kindness is showing love to someone else. I believe this kindness is the cure to violence and hatred around the world."

My daughter and I personally met Marianne Williamson at the conference. She was very nice to us. I had met her seven years earlier at Brendon Burchard's very first public seminar in a three-ring circus tent in Long Beach, California. I was his very first student in 2008. Nobody knew him then. Now he has five million followers on Facebook.

I met Brendon Burchard a second time this past April (2017) in Las Vegas, Nevada. He was super happy to see me, remembering when we met. He hugged me two times. Then I introduced myself to his mother, Mama B. She was carrying her little dog, which didn't bark once during the eight-hour seminar lecture. What an amazing experience. He now has two million students.

Dr. Wayne Dyer said, "Brendon Burchard accomplished more in three years than any of us at Hay House in thirty years."

Marianne Williamson is an authority on *A Course in Miracles*, which I have been studying for five years at the Osher Lifelong Learning Institute (OLLI) at California State University, Fullerton.

I love *A Course in Miracles* work. It is also my favorite study group.

Two very important questions are examined:

1. Where will love have me be?
2. Where will love have me go?

The present moment is where love is. Love is everything and everything is love. Miracles happen when we love each other. Remember to spread love in everything you do.

A Course in Miracles says, "Forgiveness paints a picture of the world where suffering is over, loss becomes impossible, and anger makes no sense. Attack is gone and madness has an end."

I learned from the Oakbrook IONS conference to work on being a better listener. Listening is even more powerful than talking. Listen to the voice in your heart. That is the feeling in my awareness that I keep alive on a daily basis.

A Course in Miracles" continually says that what is not fear is only love. What is not love is only fear and nothing else. What matters here is to have loving thoughts grounded in love and to remember that we are only here to love. The miracles are the shifting from fear to love. Not giving love to others is only fear and nothing else. Love is the answer for every problem.

As a three-time cancer survivor, I learned from *A Course in Miracles* that nothing is outside of me. Love is where natural healing and balance occurs within me. The cure is me! The cure is you! We need to get over ourselves and our egos.

My assignment for the rest of my physical life is to spread love, gratitude, compassion, and kindness to family, friends, students, and the community. Let go of things that do not serve me: Let go, let god! And be grateful. I hope it is your assignment too.

I took the "Conscious Aging" workshop, based on Kathleen Erickson Freeman's book of the same title, to develop wisdom, connect with others, and celebrate life. The author focused on seniors who have retired or who are soon to be retired and what the meaning of life is when you have about 25 percent of your life left. I learned to show self-compassion, practice forgiveness, and create a new vision of aging. (For more information go to www. Noetic.org.)

What I learned most in the ten years of having the Wisdom Healing Circle was that love and music are the most powerful things in life. I feel that music is love and love is music.

After leading the Wisdom Healing Circles for a decade, I ended this community group on February 15, 2016. I felt we'd had a good run, and my heart told me it was time to do other things in my life like write a book and teach at OLLI, where I have been teaching wisdom healing for three years. It was all worth it. We all learned many things and shared many experiences, adventures, and the stories of our lives. So be it. All things begin, and all things end. And so it is.

Chapter 7

Teaching Is My Greatest Joy

My career in teaching really started when I was fifteen years old. I had my first job as a Fuller Brush Man, selling cleaning products door-to-door, cold calling. It was not an easy job at first because people would slam the door in my face and tell me to get lost. Some people can be so cold and mean. Once I got used to it, I really liked it. I was making about eight to nine dollars an hour and that was in 1969. The minimum hourly wage, if you even had a job, was $1.65.

My friends from high school could not believe I was making that kind of money. They said, "Can you get me a job?" I started my teaching profession by training ten to fifteen friends to sell for Fuller Brush. Not too long afterward, they all quit because they could not sell. I believe most people cannot sell, and I feel that I was born to sell and to teach.

My teaching skills really heated up when I went to work as the first solar energy salesman in the United States. Once I got established as the number one salesman in the U.S., I started to train fifty or so sales people. I believe the reason most salespeople cannot sell is that they do not have the enthusiasm. And the most important thing is that you have to know how to close the sale. It is not everything; it is the only thing. Again, salespeople come and go. Life is a revolving door.

My sales training teaching went into even higher gear, in 1994, when I worked for the McKesson Corporation. They sold the brand named Sparkletts Water at the time. I became a super trainer and teacher of selling and cold calling to commercial accounts, door-to-door, for multiple water products. I was responsible for personally training three hundred salespeople, most of whom came and went during my eight-year career.

When I started the Wisdom Circle as a community leader in 2005, my teaching skills began to really take focus. I enjoyed getting people to open up about their feelings, thoughts, and emotions. The real joy for me is when people start sharing their personal experiences and stories about their own personal lives. Everyone has a story, and storytelling is very powerful. For me, it doesn't get better than that.

I will never forget my dear friend Patti bringing a homeless friend to the Wisdom Healing Circle on the night our guest speaker was the assistant director of a homeless shelter.

There were thirty-five people at my house that night. Eventually, the homeless person told her story about living in her car for over a year. Everyone was so touched by her story, that for the very first time, a collection plate went around the room collecting several hundred dollars in donations for Patti's friend.

The homeless person then got in touch with the guest speaker, who helped her with permanent housing. What a true story of the power of storytelling. I am very grateful when I can touch lives through my teaching and help inspire, encourage, motivate, and make the difference in people's lives. This makes it for me more than anything else I have done in my life.

My love of teaching and opening hearts carried over to OLLI. The institute has been around for thirty-seven years, and it is a learning program for retired and semi-retired adults. It is a very important part of the California State University, Fullerton, operating under the guidance of the University Extended Education program under the CSUF Auxiliary Services Corporation.

OLLI-CSUF has more than 150 classes and more than 1,700 students, with no homework, no tests, and no grades. How do you like that? No pressure! It is a self-funded organization with only four paid employees and more than four hundred volunteers. If it were not for the beautiful souls—including me—who volunteer their time, energy, and efforts, there would be no institute. What does that tell us about the power of volunteerism? My hope here is that more of you will volunteer in your communities, give back to others, and expect nothing. I believe that is the true meaning of service to others.

In 2013, when I went to an OLLI open house, I was not yet an OLLI student. We gathered around the table for the mind, body, spirit series from *A Course in Miracles* study group. I had heard of *A Course in Miracles* before. I began talking to several people who asked if I was a new student and what was I doing in my life at that time.

I told them I was a community group leader and that I held a Wisdom Circle with guest speakers at my home once a month. Then the question came: What is a Wisdom Circle? Of course, I explained in detail what it was. More people surrounded me with curiosity.

Then a distinguished gentleman said he wanted to talk to me when I was finished talking to the group. When I went over to him, he said, "I am the vice president of programs for OLLI California State University, Fullerton." Then, to my total surprise, he asked, "Do you want to be a teacher here?"

I was in shock because I was not even a student there. My immediate answer was, "Yes, I am interested in being a teacher." His next question was, "What is the name of your class?" Without hesitation I said, "Wisdom healing." He responded, "I like that."

He told me he would set up a board meeting where I would be interviewed by ten to fifteen board members. "Come prepared because they're going to ask you some very important and tough questions. If you pass the interview process, then you can become a teacher."

I could not believe what had just happened. I believe in miracles. Yes!

When I showed up for the interview with the board members, I was a bit nervous but confident. Their first question was, "Why do you want to be a teacher here? And why would anyone want to take your class?"

My answers were direct and to the point: "I want to be a teacher here so I can inspire, encourage, and motivate people to practice wisdom healing. I will teach how to heal our hearts, minds, bodies, and spirits. We can heal ourselves by our thoughts, feelings, and emotions. My students will learn how to practice awareness, consciousness, mindfulness, and self-healing techniques for better health and wellness."

I went on to list the lessons I would discuss:

- Having love for ourselves
- Having love for each other
- Turning fear-based thoughts into love
- Having love for nature and the planet
- Being grateful and living in gratitude
- Practicing sound healing
- Accepting and honoring oneself as the key to a happy life
- Being in service to others with no expectations
- Being humble and leaving one's ego at the door

The panel's second question was, "Why would anyone want to take your class?"

I said, "Because I know that most people, no matter what their age, want to live their lives with quality, not quantity. I will teach students how to learn, grow, and heal and to be able to appreciate their lives more." I explained that by practicing gratitude on a daily basis, their lives would get better.

As soon as I said that, the board members offered me the teaching position. I was elated, proud, and grateful. Again, I believe in miracles! I am especially grateful to that vice president of programs. I have been teaching at the university for three and a half years now. Wow! Where does the time go?

I love teaching; it's a gift that keeps giving. I love to see students make a shift and change in their lives right in front of my eyes. They become more open-minded, more free-spirited, and more open to the possibilities of life. I also see them become more kind and loving to this beautiful world. I want to give my time, effort, and energy to make the world a better place. I give thanks to all my students, for I live in love and gratitude. I tell my students that "in spirit" means "inspiration," and when we are inspired, we create.

My student and Coordinator for my Wisdom Healing class, David Cortez, introduced to me his friend Prany Sananikone, the director of diversity relations and educational programs at the University of California, Irvine. Sananikone, who is known for his wisdom, loves to ask lots of questions. I learned a lot from him, and he became a guest speaker in my wisdom healing class.

He taught "Mindfulness and Mortality." His topic is about living in the present—right here, right now—and not being afraid of death. He makes three very important points:

- Do not complicate your life; make it simple.
- Have quality of life, not quantity of life.
- Have dignity and integrity in your life.

Wisdom healing is about awakening to whatever stage of life we find ourselves in. I believe there are four quarter stages of life:

○ *Stage 1*, newborn to twenty years old, is when we are growing up.
○ *Stage 2*, ages twenty to forty, is when we are working to develop our careers.

- ○ *Stage 3*, ages forty to sixty, is when we have worked hard at our careers and have raised our families and developed some wisdom.
- ○ *Stage 4*, ages sixty to eighty and beyond, is when some of us are retired or semi-retired and hopefully have learned a lot more wisdom and awareness about life. At this stage, we hope to be living in the present moment and be grateful for what is important in our lives now.

I teach these life changing concepts in Wisdom Healing class in the hope that students will empower themselves throughout *all* stages of their lives. I teach how to not live in fear, to live with love, in this present moment without judgment, while focusing on one thing at a time only, avoiding multi-tasking:

- • *Observation*—What do people in the United States and around the world feel about aging and dying with grace? Shall we face our ends with courage and dignity? Why do people fear death? It is the unknown factor of when and how people all pass away. We must celebrate life now in this moment, be grateful, and continue to practice love and happiness. We all need to create inner and outer peaceful ways of life.
- • *Mindfulness*—Be mindful of your faith and belief system. Practice compassion in action to yourself and others. We need to accept and be in peace, as we all are going to pass away from this physical body.

- *Motivation*—What gives meaning and purpose to our lives on a daily basis is that we are grateful to look forward to each day and that we are alive and breathing. There are always messages and signals from the universe teaching us. We want to learn gratitude, positive attitude, Law of Attraction, vibrational sound healing, as well as follow our dreams, practice affirmations, and manifest our dreams and daily meditations.

I find that remembering powerful quotes really heals and motivates me. Here are some of my favorites.

Mindfulness means paying attention in a particular way, on purpose, in the present moment non-judgmentally.
—Jon Kabat-Zinn, professor and author,

The most precious gift we can offer anyone is our attention. When mindfulness embraces those we love, they will bloom like flowers.
—Thich Nhat Hanh, Buddhist monk

If you are depressed, you are living in the past. If you are anxious, you are living in the future. If you are at peace, you are living in the present.
—Lao-tzu, Taoist

Watch your thoughts, they become words. Watch your words, they become actions. Watch your actions, they become habit. Watch your habit, it becomes your destiny.
—Lao-tzu, Taoist

Here, too, is my list of wisdoms:

- Let go of complaining.
- Let go of blaming.
- Let go of explaining
- Let go of comparing.
- Let go of competing.
- Let go of judgments.
- Let go of anger.
- Let go of regrets.
- Let go of worrying.
- Let go of guilt.
- Let go of fear.
- Have a super good laugh at least once a day.

Another man I met at OLLI is Dr. Ronald W. Jue. Dr. Jue is a gifted soul who practices compassion and love. He visited my class, and I was amazed by his wisdom, awareness, and mindfulness immediately upon meeting him. I got to know Ron as a friend and a man of humility and peace.

I am very grateful to know Dr. Ronald Jue. He is such an inspiration to me. I invited him to be a guest speaker in my wisdom healing class in 2015. I had forty-four students that day, the most ever to attend a single class. His topic was mindfulness, and he got very high reviews for his lecture. I recommended Dr. Jue to OLLI-CSUF to be a teacher of mindfulness. He was asked to be an instructor for the summer of 2017. Thank you, Ron, for being my friend and my teacher.

I would also like to add a special note here to say that my best friend at OLLI-CSUF, Mark Geller, just passed away in December 2016. Mark was a student in my wisdom healing class. He was not just a great student at OLLI; he was also a great friend. I had the privilege of knowing Mark for three and a half years. He was a very friendly, kind, and caring man. He will be missed by all.

All of you know now that I enjoy telling the true stories of what I learned from love, courage, and wisdom. Another experience I want to share with you is that I have two beautiful students in my wisdom healing class named Sandy and Linda Freud. Sandy always shares with us his words of wisdom. My favorite quotes from him are, "Trust is a must!"; "Paralysis of the analysis"; and "Live, laugh, and love, and put love first."

Sandy's uncle was Dr. Sigmund Freud, who is known as the father of psychiatry and psychoanalysis. He invented the terms: *id, ego,* and *superego*. These aspects of the human personality are part of Dr. Freud's psychoanalytic personality theory. According to Freud, they combine to create the complex behavior of human beings:

1. *Id*—the basic part of the personality. It wants instant gratification for our wants and needs. If these needs or wants are not met, a person becomes tense and/or anxious.
2. *Ego*—the part of the personality that deals with reality. The ego deals with the realities of trying to

meet the desires of the id in a way that is socially acceptable in the world. This may mean delaying gratification and helping to get rid of the tension the id feels if a desire is not met right away. The ego recognizes that other people have needs and wants too and that being selfish is not always good for us in the long run.

3. *Superego*—the part of the personality that adds morals. The superego develops last and is based on morals and judgments about who is right and wrong. Even though the superego and the ego may reach the same decision about anything, the superego reasons for any decision that is more based on moral judgments, while the ego's decisions are based more on what others will think of you and/ or consequences of what the actions of others could be. (For additional information, see http:// examples.yourdictionary.com/examples-of-id-ego-and-superego.html.)

With a better understanding of the three parts of the human personality, I have developed a better relationship with all my students, including Sandy and Linda Freud. I have also gained a better appreciation of his uncle's teaching on this important subject. The ego is often brought up in spiritual classes, especially in the *A Course in Miracles* study group and in my wisdom healing class.

If your id, ego, superego are out of control with fear, I recommend that you spread more love to others. However, before you can do that, you have to learn to love yourself. If you do not love yourself or only love yourself a little bit, I know of a technique that will help you tremendously.

Go in front of a mirror each day, look at yourself, and say, "I love you!" seven times. Then hold your arms across your body and tell the little child inside yourself that has been hurt and rejected, "I love the child within myself." This should be your daily affirmation until you do love yourself.

You will likely need to practice this for quite some time because you could have spent many, many years not loving yourself, or perhaps even your whole life.

I have experienced this myself over the years. I believe fear today is contagious, and it is an epidemic. It is spreading like wildfire all over the United States and the world. Let us not buy into the fear that is out there. Do not give it energy. If you give it energy, you will only get more fear.

Please spread love, kindness, and compassion to your family, friends, fellow students, coworkers, and other people you meet. That will increase the vibration and energy of the world to an energy of love. Please practice this daily, my friends.

We all dream while we sleep. Before writing this, I had just awoken from a dream about the forty-fifth President of the United States, Donald J. Trump. I dreamed that President Trump and I had five hamburgers and French fries that were hanging out of our mouths as we ate them. I think I saw that in a big game commercial.

What I learned from my dream is that the food symbolized love. My hope here is that the president, the country, and our world can be filled with more peace and love for ourselves and spread it to everyone, everywhere. I wish you all lots of love and peace in your lives, just like Ringo Starr of the Beatles has been consistently saying for fifty-three years now.

Another thing I want to mention is how important it is to teach my students in wisdom healing and in the art of sound healing. It is an extremely valuable practice. We do a drum circle, just like the North American native Indian people have done for hundreds of years. We sit in a circle, and I play a drum the size of a very large plate. Then we practice the singing crystal bowl, which sounds like a wine glass that you rub your finger around to make a humming noise. It makes you feel balanced, grounded, and relaxed.

Then I play the holistic percussion turtle, which is a steel drum that is cut perfectly and tuned to the ideal of 133-hertz sound. When I play this instrument, my students tell me that they feel so relaxed and like they are in heaven. The whole room vibrates when I play my three sound healing musical instruments. It is very important that we practice sound healing on a regular basis for calm, peaceful, and blissful relaxation.

Chapter 8

My Soul Mate, Rainbow Turtle

I met my soul mate, Rainbow Turtle, on July 29, 2012. I knew she was different right away because she was childlike and spiritually enlightened. Being a spiritually aware person is very important to me on my journey of life. She is playful, likes to laugh a lot, and is fun to be with. I enjoyed our first date, and we were spiritually aligned.

Our second date was an interview at her music, dance, and performing arts studio. I knew it went well, because four hours went by as if it were thirty minutes. That is how it always is with my Rainbow Turtle. Being with her for seven hours and talking about the meaning of spiritual thoughts, feelings, and emotions seems to go by in one hour. That is how you know you are with the right person.

After three years together, my soul mate Rainbow Turtle and I broke up because of unhealed contrasts and issues from our pasts. We were apart for nine months, and then a miracle happened. I was driving home on November 26, 2015, which was Thanksgiving Day, and I saw a rainbow over Carbon Canyon in Chino Hills, California, after it rained. Rainbows in my area are extremely rare sights.

When I got home from my daughter Sarah's house, I texted Rainbow and told her that I saw her somewhere over the mountain. I then talked to her on the phone that night, and we agreed to meet for tea at Starbucks, the same place where we had met for the very first time four years earlier.

We had a wonderful time. Rainbow took me out to dinner, and we celebrated seeing each other. She then gave me ten presents and said she had never stopped loving me during our breakup. This experience really touched and melted my heart.

When we went outside, it was very cold that night and we were the only people in the parking lot around 10:30 p.m. Then another miracle happened. We heard the song "Up Where We Belong" by Joe Cocker and Jennifer Warns from the movie *An Officer and A Gentleman* starring Richard Gere and Debra Winger. Since we both love music, that song touched our hearts and spoke to us from the spiritual awareness that we share.

Well, the next miracle was that we got back together that night. And, oh, what a night it was! December 2, 2015! We will never forget this experience of heaven on Earth at that moment in time. We all know that everything in our lives happens for our benefit. We believe in miracles. Yes!

Our relationship has grown over the years. We enjoy the same things and have a love of music, theater, concerts, plays, the arts, lectures, conferences and conventions, and traveling the world. The most important thing is that we are best friends. It does not get any better than soul mates who are best friends. We are twin flames coming from the same place. We have the same thoughts at the same time. We finish each other's sentences because we are both heart centered, two totally evolved people who have become one.

We recently had an amazing experience. We were both sleeping soundly together and had a nightmare at the very same moment. We both woke up screaming at the very same time with the same exact nightmare. The nightmare was about my Rainbow Turtle being violated by another person, an intuition of how 2016 would end. A few days later, her music, dance, and performing arts studio was broken into and burglarized. If this is not an incredible experience, then I do not know what is. I have never had this happen in my entire life. We are so connected that our dreams are just as connected as we are.

The love, respect, and care we have for one another is a beautiful thing. We both live in love and gratitude for everything we have together in this life. I really appreciate my Rainbow Turtle. Just like I manifested her in my HeartMath class five years ago, she is the sweetest, kindest, gentlest, and most tender woman I have ever met.

All I wanted in my life was to meet a woman like her because I have met many women in my life who were abusive and mean and who took advantage of me. My Rainbow Turtle never does that. She does not try to change or fix me. She accepts me just the way I am. She does not judge me; she just loves me.

I want my readers to know the meaning behind the name I gave my Rainbow Turtle. The reason I call her Rainbow is because the colors of the rainbow are so beautiful in nature, the wonders of the world on full display. I believe rainbows form when sunlight hits the rainwater in the very same moment, causing a prism of colors of light to be transmitted to Earth. My Rainbow Turtle is so full of life and love and has the best attitude of any person I have ever met.

The reason I call her Turtle is because these beautiful beings go with the flow and are good navigators. They stay calm under pressure, are well traveled, and think in the long term. They do not make many mistakes because they take their time. What is most important about turtles is that they live a long time and age gracefully. One more thing about turtles is that they retreat inside of their shells for protection from a fast-paced world while they move slowly towards their goals.

Now you all know why I call my soul mate Rainbow Turtle. At the exact moment that I wrote this passage, I received a love message from my Rainbow Turtle, saying, "I am so happy you are writing this book, Marty, and I believe it is a cathartic healing and fulfilling to share your love, courage, and wisdom with others and the world." When I read that, my heart started to vibrate with a beautiful feeling of love and gratitude for my soul mate and for the fact that we have this connection on a consistent basis.

We live in heaven on Earth, right here, right now, because we have a very strong spiritual awareness of who we are and what our life purpose is. This is the glue that has built a strong foundation in our relationship.

I have a wonderful story to share with you. My Rainbow Turtle and I went to the Conscious Living Expo at the Los Angeles International Airport Hilton Hotel. This is an amazing place, and I felt energy there that day. It is the same hotel where my brothers and I had my father's memorial a few years before. I felt my dad's spirit and energy when my Rainbow Turtle and I were coming out of the elevator at the expo. I felt a very powerful energy field come over my body. My entire mind, body, and soul were vibrating at a very high speed all over my being. The vision spirit message I got was that my Rainbow Turtle is my forever life partner. This was a very profound and incredible experience that I will never forget.

Another incredible experience happened to me about two

weeks ago. I call it an epiphany. I was making dinner for my soul mate when I had this very powerful vision.

I am being very truthful and honest with you, readers, when I say that I heard God's voice say, "I am God and this is what I look like." I could not believe my eyes. God was a rectangle. The figure looked exactly 50 percent animal, like a dog, and 50 percent human. The body had all white fur with black spikes, with a small head, arms, and legs. I immediately drew a picture of it to the exact specifications that I had seen. Because energy is everything and everything is energy, I believe our Higher Power is half-animal and half-human.

I was overwhelmed with excitement and wonder. I have never seen anything like this in my entire life. I believe this was a message from my highest power. This profound experience was my teacher for my highest good.

Just as powerful as this experience, three to four days later, I went to my soul mate Rainbow Turtle's music, dance, and performing arts studio to pick her up for a concert that night. When I came through the door—she has a little tiny window that looks into her piano room so that she can see when children and parents come in for a piano lesson—I was completely surprised and shocked to find that she was wearing a white fur jacket with black spikes that I had never seen in the five years I had known her.

She said the jacket had been sitting in her closet for a year and that she had never worn it with me before. I could not believe my eyes again. Her jacket was the exact picture I had envisioned and drawn three days before. Remember, I do not believe in accidents or coincidences. I believe in synchronicity. Everything happens for a reason and for our benefit, no matter what the experience is.

The wisdom here is that animals, trees, flowers, wildlife, and all of nature are from God. They are God's gifts to us. They are our teachers. Dogs especially live in the present moment, give unconditional love 24-7, and do not judge you. Don't you think we humans should learn from animals and nature to shift our awareness, consciousness, and mindfulness to come from unconditional love for each other?

My hope here is that all of us practice love, gratitude, compassion, kindness, and peace toward each other every day. But we all forget and slide backward. The key is then getting back on track. Please remind yourself to change and shift your thoughts, feelings, and emotions back to love.

My Rainbow Turtle and I have traveled to Cancun, Mexico, and to Hawaii two times, as well as to Italy, Budapest, Hungary, Vienna, Austria, Prague, The Czech Republic, and Germany. We took each other to Spain and Portugal this past summer. I love traveling with her because she is so easy to be with. She is the most easy-going person I have ever met. It is important to me that we tell each other every day that we love one another. As we all know, love is most important thing in the infinity of this universe.

One more thing my Rainbow Turtle and I learned about

my life is all the different kinds of women and men I have known. Here is the list of the four unique types of people I have experienced:

1. *The "mixed fruit salad of girls"*—My soul mate likes to call them this because of the many women I have had in my life.

2. *The "spider web" of men and women in my experience*— What I mean by this is that some women and men have taken advantage of my kindness and generosity and used, abused, and violated me in different ways. I forgive everyone who has done this in my life, because I chose these people and I attracted it.

3. *The "corpses" of people are the walking dead*—These people are unresponsive and not in touch with their thoughts, feelings, and emotions. They are not romantically available and are cold as ice. The lights are on, but nobody is home. I will continue to pray for these souls, and my hope is that one day they will become enlightened beings.

4. *The "sweet and loving" people of the world*—These people are caring and compassionate and come from love, kindness, mindfulness, joy, gratitude, and peace.

I want to say thank you to my Rainbow Turtle for loving me and for our mutual honoring of each other just the way we are. I have learned, grown, and healed so much from your being in my life. I love you, the whole world, and beyond.

Chapter 9

Love and Gratitude

I believe that love and gratitude are the two most important words in this world. If you have them and practice both, then you will have everything you will ever need or want in your life.

Without them, I feel that we will suffer greatly and live our lives unfulfilled, lonely, and empty. We can all have love and gratitude in our lives if we just practice them on a daily basis, and I mean with a conscientious effort. My advice to you is to start making a gratitude journal and write down everything you are grateful for, not just on Thanksgiving, birthdays, and holidays but every day. Even if it is one thing, write it down, appreciate it, and be thankful. I feel that the problem is that most people take things for granted and do not practice what I am writing and talking about. We all have the power to change. The change is you!

The Beatles again had it right: "All you need is love, love. Love is all you need!" I believe love is everything and everything is love. Remember how it all starts with self-love? I know it is not easy; it is hard to change old patterns, especially since around 80 percent of what we were told about ourselves growing up was negative. Practice each and every day until it becomes a habit.

The wisdom here is that the past does not equal the future. You can start a clean slate right here, right now. All that matters is *now*—this present moment. And if you start loving yourself, then you can definitely love anybody else. We all deserve to love and to be loved. So please, start loving yourself each day so that you can then love someone else. I hope you take my advice, because I have experienced more in my sixty-three years of life than most people.

What I am most grateful for in my life is that I am a three-time cancer survivor. I live in gratitude every day that I am alive. As you remember, doctors told me that I had a 90 percent chance of dying within one year's time. I am still here eighteen years later, and I am a miracle! I beat all the odds and live each day being very thankful to God and the universe. That I get to live in this body and have a human experience is a miracle in itself. Most cells die and never become a body. Only the strongest cells live and are born.

"'Cause we are the champions of the world," just like the rock music group Queen sings. We are all miracles, and do not forget it.

When I wrote my own gratitude list, I listed fifty-three things I was grateful for. They sure add up if you pay attention and practice gratitude. Remember, no excuses like, "I don't have any time to do that." Please make the time, for it will serve you well.

I used to get mad and angry all the time, but now practicing love and gratitude, I rarely get mad or upset. The problem is that a lot of people are mad, angry, and bitter. Please stop being angry and turn it into gratitude. You will see a world of difference in your attitude. Make it an attitude of gratitude.

I want to write about all the wisdom I learned from my father. My dad and I made an investment together in a 350-unit hotel in Shell Beach, California, in the 1980s. My other partners were Carl Karcher of Carl's Jr. and William French Smith, who was secretary of the treasury under President Ronald Reagan. The investment went bankrupt, and we lost all our money.

My father felt so bad about it that he reimbursed all the money back to me plus 10 percent interest. This was the kind of man my father was. I will always love my dad and be grateful for all the wisdom I learned from him. When I was getting divorced, my dad said, "Son, you got yourself into this mess. Now get yourself out of this nightmare." I just love his words, so simple but so deep.

Getting divorced from my second wife was a very sad experience. The judge in our case said, "You two can't decide on anything when it comes to visitation of the two young children. So, because of that, Mr. Cole, you cannot see your children for three months."

This just crushed me. I had seen my two beautiful girls every day since their births. I was the one who got up for their nightly feedings and changed their diapers. I adored my children. They were ten and five years of age. To this day, I advise other divorced dads to not give up on their kids. I hope all courts give divorcing moms and dads equal rights and treatment in the future.

I got very depressed at that time, and then I saw a movie called *Mrs. Doubtfire*, starring Robin Williams and Sally Fields. Mrs. Doubtfire was a divorced man with three small children, and the judge said, "You can't see your kids because you can't hold a job." The father did whatever it took to see his kids. He dressed as a female nanny and got the job at his kids' mother's house.

Well, I was not going to become a woman to see my kids. But what I did do was go to my children's elementary school and ask if I could volunteer in each of my girls' classrooms. The principal of the school was very surprised that I had asked for a volunteer position. She said, "We've never seen a dad come to our school before and ask to volunteer. We have seen moms come before but never dads."

I got the job and volunteered for one year in my daughter Melissa's kindergarten class and my daughter Sarah's fifth grade class. I am very grateful for that experience and that I was inspired by that movie about a father's love for his children. I love my two daughters, and I am grateful for them every day of my life. They know how much I love and care for them.

I am very grateful to Fred and Frankie, who became the first Wisdom Circle participants in 2005. It started with two people, and grew to fifty-four in eleven years. I never advertised or promoted it. It grew by only word of mouth. We had so many great times and great experiences. I am thankful to the three hundred different people who came and went.

I had an amazing experience on December 4, 2004. My dad was very sick and in failing health. I went to visit him with my three brothers in Vista, California. My brother Steve stayed overnight with me at my house. The television in my bedroom was never hooked up. It is just there for decoration only.

At 5:15 a.m., when I was sound asleep, that unplugged TV turned on by itself and was super loud with snow on the screen. I suddenly woke up, jumped out of bed, and was really scared and freaked out. I thought I had seen a ghost.

I had never been more frightened. I finally calmed down twenty minutes later and went back to sleep.

At 7:30 that same morning, there was a knock at my bedroom door and I was awakened again, this time by my brother Steve. He said, "Marty, I have some really bad news. I just got a call from our brother Mike that our dad passed away this morning at 5:15 a.m."

What this means to me is that my dad was communicating to me through the television to say good-bye. Many psychics have told me that loved ones who pass away can communicate with you through electricity and water, especially if they loved you and were close to you.

This experience with the TV turning itself on when it was not plugged in happened again for the next two days in a row after my dad passed, at exactly 5:15 a.m. each time.

I believe that my father is now my spirit guide. All I know is I miss my dad very much. I will always love him on this side and on the other side of life.

Once my father passed away, he was instrumental in helping me with my mother. I immediately needed to find another place for her to live. She had been displaced, and I only had two days to find her a new home.

I went to fifteen different board and care residential facilities. These places were very bad, and it looked to me like there were dead people just lying in bed. I knew

I wanted to get the best possible care provider for my mother. I was getting very frustrated and was running out of time.

I was so stressed out that I just parked my car in San Marcos, California, and sat there for several moments. Then I talked to my dad on the other side. I said, "Dad, please help me right now to find a place for Mom to live." I remember his exact words: "Don't worry, son, everything is going to be okay!" I heard my father's voice. I kid you not.

I knew at that exact moment that my dad was my spirit guide. A spirit guide is a person who has passed to the other side and who is there for you. I believe it only happens when you ask your spirit guide for help. I am telling you nothing but the truth, so help me God. After two minutes, I looked up and saw a sign that read, "Assisted Living and Alzheimer's Dementia Care Facility." I could not believe my eyes.

I went into the assisted care center and talked to the director of sales. I asked if there were any rooms available. She said they only had one room left. Then she asked, "What is the name of the person you are trying to place, and what relationship are they to you?"

I answered, "My mother's name is Dorothy Cole."

She said, "That name sounds familiar."

I said, "How is that possible?"

She then looked in her desk drawer and pulled out a lot of photographs of older individuals. Then to my shock and surprise, she said, "Is this a picture of your mother?"

I said, "Yes!" I could not believe it.

She told me that she used to work at another care center and that she knew my mother. You talk about synchronicity and miracles, well, they both happened at the same time and in same place. Again, do you believe in miracles? Yes! I undoubtedly do! Thank you, Dad, for being my spirit guide!

And that is where my mother lived until she passed away on December 11, 2011, at the age of ninety-four.

If I am having a bad day, and all of us have a bad day once in a while, I change my thoughts, feeling, and emotions and start to look at things differently. I say to myself, look at all the things I am grateful for in my life. When I see it another way, everything changes for the good. I hope you try it. What do you have to lose?

Let me tell you about my younger brother Phil. He is the sweetest, most gentle guy you will ever meet. My brother Phil was very supportive to me when I was having a very difficult time during my second divorce. He came to my house just to be there for me and give me love and support.

Phil, I really appreciate everything you did at the time. I want to also thank Phil for managing my daughters' trust accounts for college costs and living expenses. A big shout out to you, Phil, for taking care of my family estate, as well as the Cole Family Partnership. I love you very much, brother.

I wanted to save the best for last: My daughters, Sarah and Melissa, and I went on a trip to Switzerland, Italy, and Greece in the summer of 2014. I got very sick on the trip. I came down with a severe upper respiratory lung infection, and I had asthma as well. Either of these health problems can kill anyone.

I had a very difficult time breathing because I was so congested, and my nose was completely stuffed up. During the middle of the night in Lake Como, Italy, I could not breathe for about five minutes and was gasping for air. I thought I was going to die.

My daughter Sarah heard me in distress and came to my rescue with my asthma inhaler. I was then able to get a small amount of air into my lungs. I want to say, "Thank you with all my heart, Sarah, because you saved my life!"

On the same trip, the same emergency happened a second time, this time on a cruise ship to the Greek islands. "Sarah, you saved my life two times. I love you with all my heart." I do not think I will be taking a sea cruise again anytime soon.

The next thing I am grateful for in my life are the ten shrines I have in my home. They display the symbols of the rhinoceros, the lighthouse, Buddha, the owl, and the wisdom sayings of the universe. I had a dream in 2003, and in the dream, I manifested turning an empty room into a lighthouse room.

The next morning, I woke up, took action, and made it happen. Today, I have three thousand figurines, photos, images, and collectible lighthouses in one room. When you dream it, create it! Take action in your life. Do not live in fear. Live in love. Thank you to all, and make it a great life.

What I learned most in 2016 and 2017 is in regard to technology and its impact on communication. I feel we have gone way overboard in the how we communicate with others. Today we communicate by e-mail, text messages, Facebook, Twitter, Instagram, etc. We are not talking in person to each other at all, and even on a cell phone or via a landline. Most people communicate only digitally, which is very sad and unfortunate.

In a CSUF auditorium, 203 students ages eighteen to twenty-four were on a class break. I observed two hundred students on cell phones, laptops, or tablets. There was no in-person verbal communication happening between them.

I feel that we are on a dangerous path. People are becoming alienated, separated, and isolated from each other. I see that many people are afraid to even pick up a phone call because they do not want to deal with real people. As a result, we are becoming more isolated from each other. I believe that the majority of people are now addicted to their cell phones and devices mainly for Internet usage.

I hope we start communicating again in the old-fashioned way—by talking to each other face-to-face or on the phone in real time, hearing each other's voices, right here and right now, in the present moment.

Also, I see that robots, drones, and driverless cars are taking over our country and the world. If this continues, more and more people will lose their jobs. What is this world coming to with this dangerous and cold technology and artificial intelligence?

Again, I hope we can change this by spreading more love and not fear to each other. I am asking you, please, to practice more love, kindness, compassion, and peace for yourselves and others on this planet. Hopefully, we can save this beautiful Earth and the universe from a negative future. I thank you for practicing these ways. I wish you all love and gratitude always.

Over the last couple years, I've learned a lot from some of the relationships I've had. I've been friends with these men and women for anywhere between ten to forty-five years. What I have learned is that I have outgrown some of these souls for many different reasons. I would mostly say that my spiritual journey has taken me on a different path.

I passionately felt that I needed to disconnect from about ten to fifteen of these old friends because they were negative, toxic, blamers, complainers, and played the victim role. Letting go of these people has really empowered and energized me. I felt complete freedom and satisfaction that I did this for my health and growth as a person.

The wisdom here is if people in your life are bringing you pain, suffering, and drama, you may want to make changes to be more at peace. When you let go of people who do not serve you, your health and well-being will improve and you will feel empowered. My hope here is that you will have the courage to take action, change your life, and make the best life possible.

I learned to say no. It's freeing. You can stop being a doormat to people. There will be people who try to take advantage of you and use up your time, money, energy, and generosity. It is important to put up your boundaries and borders to protect yourself. Do not feel guilty when you say no. Saying no will help you feel empowered and more confident. We need to say no to loved ones and friends in situations where it doesn't feel right to go along with and where our safety or security is at risk.

We need to practice moderation in everything we do. We must not go overboard or underboard in our behaviors and lifestyles. Even do moderation with moderation. I feel if you can accomplish this, your life will be more balanced, grounded, and peaceful. You will have less stress and be more at ease.

If we do not practice this moderation wisdom, then life will have more fear and disease and there will be more out of control situations in your experiences. Mr. Arnold Beckman of Beckman Instruments told me this. He lived until he was 101 years old, so he sure practiced what he preached. Arnold Beckman also said, "When you are in business as the manager or leader, hire good people and then stay out of their way and let them do their jobs." I think this is extremely good advice. Don't you?

When I have inspiration in my life, I become much more creative. Inspiration gives me a lot of momentum and my body starts to vibrate down my seven chakras. My awareness and mindfulness operates on a much higher energy level. I feel so euphoric. I can accomplish so much more in my life to help others. I have learned to be open to experiencing this feeling because it is very powerful and life becomes more meaningful and has purpose. My hope is that you stay inspired in your life and create the best life you possibly can.

Haile Selassie, former emperor of Ethiopia said, "History teaches us that unity is strength and cautions us to submerge and overcome our differences in the quest for common goals." To me, this means we should accept each other's differences and unite as one. We all are connected. No one is better than you, and you are no better than anyone else. I saw the emperor in person, with my brother Mike, at the University of California Los Angeles at the Pauley Pavilion in 1967. I will never forget the wisdom and presence of Emperor Haile Selassie of Ethiopia.

Love, blessings, gratitude, compassion, kindness, mindfulness, joy, and peace to you and your family. Thank you!

I love you all.

Epilogue

I have had the good fortune of meeting many famous people. I heard Donald Trump speak in person in 2004 at "The Business Success Motivation Conference" in Anaheim, California. He said, "As long as you're going to think, think big!" Now he's the president of the United States.

With this Las Vegas, Nevada shooting massacre on Sunday, October 1, 2017, I again want to take this opportunity for all of us to please spread more love and peace to everyone and everywhere to get this violence to cease.

I am not into religion or politics. In the name of religion and politics, one billion people throughout history have been killed. I do not want to be a part of either. I see how with this election our country and world is sharply divided. This makes me want to spread more love and gratitude. In military school, I was baptized against my will, nearly drowned, traumatized, and forced to participate in a different religion each year, which I did not want at all. I believe we are all free to think, believe, and dream however we choose.

So with this 2016 election, I had a great opportunity to honor my own spiritual practices. I reminded myself not to be in judgment of anyone, to have the awareness of miracles, and to do my daily spiritual meditations. I stay positive and hopeful for our world and receive the miracles that are all around me every day.

I always focus on maintaining a positive attitude toward life. I will always be optimistic, no matter what happens in our country or in the world. My hope here is that you, my readers, will please spread more love, peace, compassion, kindness, and mindfulness to your families, friends, fellow students, coworkers, and the people you meet. Let us make this world a better place for you and me. Love, blessings, and gratitude.

Do not live in fear. Live in love. Thank you all!

Gratitude

Never underestimate the power of gratitude.
An attitude of gratitude is the never-ending prayer.
You are my morning light that makes
me forget the dark night.
I am grateful for all your gifts,
As your love gives me my biggest lift.
So let gratitude give you the best attitude,
When you're feeling you are getting the healing.
When you're having your emotions,
Is when you're in motion.
When you have your laughter is what you're after.
It's all about gratitude of love and the love of gratitude

—Marty Cole, May 11, 2015

Listen to the Voice in Your Heart

Listen to the voice in your heart.
It will get you where you want to start.
Follow your heart and not your head
and then you will have the best part.
Your heart is where your thoughts,
feelings, and emotions
are near and not far.
Live in the here and now from the start.
Listen to the voice in your heart.
It will get you where you want to start.
Follow your heart and not your head
and then you will have the best part.
Listen to the voice in your heart!
Listen to the voice in your heart!
Listen to voice in your heart!
Always start with love in your heart!

—Marty Cole, December 15, 2016

I Want to Feel the Love Tonight

When you are down and out,
I just want to feel the love tonight.
It will bring you up and make you feel all right.
Don't forget to give love and receive joy.
It's what I'm talking about.
Just love me tonight.
And it feels all right.
Forget your sorrows and
Don't worry about tomorrow.
When you're feeling the blues,
Just think about the gratitude
And then you will have the best attitude.
That's what I'm talking about.
Just love me tonight!
And it feels all right!
And forget your sorrows
And don't worry about tomorrow.

—Marty Cole, June 23, 2014

The Lighthouse

Captain by the Sea, it is 1983!
He loves fish because it is a lovely dish.
The keeper of the light never keeps it out of sight.
The seeds of the sea are all that you need.
It is an ocean of white healing light
That goes into the dark night.
He has the best attitude because he lives in gratitude.
The man by the sea is looking as fine as can be.
He comes from love in his heart from the very start.
It's all about love, so do not fear, my dear.
Back in '83, it was a very good year.
It was all about selling the sun, which
for me made it more fun.
My life has been the best. That's why I left the rest.
I rate my life as great.
I have the best attitude because I live in gratitude.
My purpose is to serve others. That's
why I love all the mothers.
My goal is to spread love and peace so
we can get violence to cease.
It's all about love, my dear.
So let's stop all the fear.

—Marty Cole, March 7, 2017

About the Author

Wisdom Circle

Marty Cole has authored a book about his life experiences. As a friend of Marty, for over 12 years, I can say that he is one of the most positive people I have ever met. When you meet Marty you immediately sense his warmth and positivity. As a member of the Wisdom Circle I experienced a group of people, from all walks of life and belief systems, who were searching to improve their day-to-day lives in an extraordinary manner. The group was very congenial and intelligent. Although we varied in our beliefs, we agreed not to discuss politics or religion.

The main focus of the Wisdom Circle was to seek out speakers who would present ways of improving life. Marty brought knowledgeable and interesting speakers, some of whom are actors, poets, psychotherapists and other professionals. We met monthly at Marty's home to share a meal and learn from the speakers and each other. In time, my daughter, Theresa, and son, Patrick, joined me after I enthusiastically spoke of what I had learned in the Wisdom Circle.

If there is a person who is actively seeking to make the world a better place through education and love, it is Marty Cole. Marty teaches at Osher Lifelong Learning Institute, OLLI, Cal State Fullerton, as he continues his mission of teaching and helping people improve their lives. Marty's experiences and his battles with cancer, prepared him for sharing the joy of living. I am convinced his book will enlighten and inform you about appreciating life and living from love and gratitude each day.

Helen M. Delaney, B.A. English, M.S. Education, Retired Teacher

Wisdom Healing Class

Marty is terrific, innovative and creative. He uses various techniques and materials to teach the class and lead worthwhile discussions. He stimulates consciousness and increases awareness. The class starts with sound healing to relax the participants: Deep breathing, a crystal "singing" bowl, a small Indian drum, and then he plays a perfectly tuned instrument that resembles a turtle shell. We love his class at "OLLI" and wouldn't miss it!

Love for ourselves and others is a basic ingredient of the class. Primary disciplines taught are being grateful and living in gratitude; turning fear-based thoughts into love; being non- judgmental and that adversity brings greatness.

Rev. S. "Sandy" and Linda Freud, OLLI Students

Recommended Resources

Name	Reference
Albert Einstein	• Saying on wall of Pieology Pizza in Fullerton, California • Any of his quotes or books·
Brendon Burchard	• Books: *The Motivation Manifesto, 9 Declarations to Claim Your Personal Power* • Website: www. brendon.com • Any of his other works
Bruce Lipton	• Books: *The Honeymoon Effect—The Science of Creating Heaven on Earth; The Biology of Belief* • Website: www. brucelipton.com • Any of his books
California State University, Fullerton Osher Lifelong Learning Institute (OLLI)	• Website: www.olli. fullerton.edu • Any of their courses

The Dalai Lama	• DVD: *Dalai Lama's Compassion in Action*
	• Website: www.dalailama.com
	• Any of his works
Deborah Jones	• Website: www.ninegates.org
Doc Childre and Howard Martin with Donna Beech	• Book: *The HeartMath Solution*
	• Website: www.heartmath.com
	• Any of their other books or conferences
Don Miguel Ruiz	• Books: *The Four Agreements; The Four Agreements Companion Book; Ripples of Wisdom*
	• Website: www.miguelruiz.com
	• Any of his other books and media
Doreen Virtue	• Workshops: *The Writers Workshop"* and any of her other workshops
	• Website: www.angeltherapy.com
	• All of her other books, media, and Angel Cards

| Eckhart Tolle | • Books: *The Power of Now; A Guide to Spiritual Enlightenment; A New Earth, Awakening to Your Life's Purpose*
• Website: www. eckhartollenow.com
• Any of his other books and lectures |
| Edgar Mitchell | • Books: *The Way of the Explorer: An Apollo Astronaut's Journey Through the Material and Mystical Worlds; Psychic Exploration*
• Video: www.youtube.com/ watch?v=uyEvWdtFzMo
• Profile: www.noetic.org/ profile/edgar-mitchell
• Any of his other books |

Esther and Jerry Hicks	• Books: *The Astonishing Power of Emotions: Let Your Feelings Be Your Guide; The Law of Attraction: The Basics of the Teachings of Abraham*
	• Website: www. abraham-hicks.com/ lawofattractionsource/ index.php
	• Any of her DVDs, CDs, workshops, and books
Foundation for Inner Peace (the organization appointed by the scribe Dr. Helen Schucman with the mandate to publish, disseminate, and discuss *A Course in Miracles*)	• Book: *A Course in Miracles*
	• Websites: www.acim.org
	• info@acim.org
	• Study groups in your area

Haile Selassie	On May 25, 1963 the Organization for African Unity (OAU) was established with a permanent headquarters in Addis Ababa, Ethiopia. Haile Selassie, emperor of Ethiopia, was selected as the first president of the OAU. See more of his acceptance speech at: http://www.blackpast. org/1963-haile-selassie- towards-african-unity#sthash. XDCDLYFf.dpuf
HeartMath	• Websites: www. HeartMath.com • www.HeartMath.org • Any of their classes, books, and DVDs
Institute of Noetic Sciences, IONS	• Website: www.noetic.org • Any of their lectures, conferences, publications, and home study groups
J. Douglas Edwards	• Book: *Closing the Deal* • See Tom Hopkins below for more information on Mr. Edwards
James Q. Simmons III	Obituary: articles.latimes. com/2005/apr/20/local/ me-simmons20

Jean Houston	• Websites: www.jeanhouston.org; jeanhoustonfoundation.org; jeanhouston.com
	• Any of her books, lectures, seminars, events, trainings, and mentoring
John R. Wooden	• Books: *The Wisdom of Wooden; The Pyramid of Success*
	• Website: www.woodencourse.com
	• Any of his other books
Jon Kabat-Zinn	• Audio: *Mindfulness Meditation—Cultivating the Wisdom of Your Body and Mind*
	• Book: *Wherever You Go, There You Are*
	• Website: www.mindfulnesscds.com
	• Any books, CDs, DVDs
Kathleen Erickson-Freeman	• Book: *IONS Conscious Aging Alliance Facilitators Guide*
	• Websites: www.noetic.org
	• www.consciousaging alliance.org

Lao Tzu (founder of philosophical Taoism, known as Laozi)	• Book: *Tao Te Ching* • Website: https:// • www.gutenberg.org/ebooks/216 • All his works
LeVar Burton (actor, producer, director, author, presenter)	• Video: *Reading Rainbows* PBS Series • Website: www.levarburton.com • Any of his films or TV shows
Louise Hay	• Books: *How to Heal Your Life*; *Heart Thoughts* • Websites: www.louisehay.com; www.healyourlife.com • www.hayhouse.com • Any of her other books, CDs, DVDs, courses, and seminars
Lynne Kitei	• Book: *The Phoenix Lights* • Website: www.thephoenixlights.net

Marilyn Schlitz and Deepak Chopra	• Book: *The Future of God* • DVD: *Death Makes Life Possible* • Websites: www.marilynschlitz.com; www.deepakchopra.com; www.chopra.com • Any of Deepak Chopra's works
Master Mingtong Gu	• Books: *Wisdom Healing Gigong; Activate and Embody Wisdom and Energy for Health; Healing and Happiness* • Website: www.chicenter.com • Any of his classes
Neale Donald Walsh	• Books: *Conversations with God* (also available as a DVD); *Bringers of the Light; How You Can Change Your Life and Change the World* • Websites: www.nealedonaldwalsch.com; www.cwg.org • All of his works and media
Richard A. Wedemeyer and Ronald W. Jue, Ph.D	• Book: *The Inner Edge: Effective Spirituality in Your Life and Work*

Robert T. Kiyosaki and Sharon Lechter	• Book: *Rich Dad, Poor Dad* • Website: www.richdad.com • All books, media, games, and seminars
Scott Robert Alexander	• Book: *Rhinoceros Success: The Secret to Charging Full Speed toward Every Opportunity* • Any of his works
Sigmund Freud	Explanation of id, ego, superego: http://examples.yourdictionary.com/examples-of-id-ego-and-superego.html
Thich Nhat Hanh	• Books: *You are Here: Discovering the Magic of the Present Moment; The Miracle of Mindfulness: An Introduction to the Practice of Meditation* • Websites: www.plumvillage.org; www.thichnhathanhfoundation.org • Any of his works

Tom Hopkins	• Book: *Mastering the Art of Selling*
	• Website: www. tomhopkins.com (this site includes J. Douglas Edwards works)
Wayne Dyer	• Books: *Excuses Be Gone: How to Change Lifelong, Self-Defeating Thinking Habits; The Essential Wayne Dyer Collection; Wishes Fulfilled; Everyday Wisdom; I Can See Clearly Now;*
	• Movie: *"The Shift"*
	• Website: www. drwaynedyer.com
	• Any of his many books and videos (see www. youtube.com)

CPSIA information can be obtained
at www.ICGtesting.com
Printed in the USA
FSHW01n2144041018